Snowing Lik

Alan Duckworth

Ashleigh Barrow Books

Snowing Like Billy –Ho!

To Sandra
with best wishes
[signature]

Alan Duckworth

Ashleigh Barrow Books

First published 2006 by Ashleigh Barrow Books

ISBN 095221735X

Ashleigh Barrow Books
Leyland

Introduction

'Magic moments' is too banal; 'epiphanies' too pretentious. I wanted to write a book about those moments in your life you always remember - the good ones that is. Those moments that are quite out of the ordinary, those moments when you are taken out of yourself, when you become at one with the experience.

They are more common in childhood. Maybe the illusion of self and separation is more easily pierced then. They often come at special times: Christmas, holidays, when the snow comes down. The earliest one for me came when I was pulled through the snow on a sledge by my Dad to see the village Christmas tree. Later it was going on holiday and seeing the sea. These are the moments that glow in the memory, when so much else is in darkness.

The nature of each one varies, and indeed some of the occurrences in this book are not magic moments at all, not in the special sense I'm trying to capture, but, as when I got the box of soldiers, or our dog had puppies, just moments of unexpected delight.

I wanted to identify them. I wanted to record them, and in doing so, the social historian in me came out and I decided to add other items; autobiographical pieces, 'what it was like' pieces: what it was like when everybody travelled by bus; when alcohol was an acquired taste; when there was free school milk; when TV first appeared; when libraries had books; when buying a house didn't mean being mortgaged beyond your means.

We live our lives for these moments. Everything we do is aimed at achieving them, capturing them, making them permanent - going on holiday; making our homes nice; creating gardens; buying a car; going out to dinner; meeting friends. All our activities are to that end, to have that experience. I'm not sure though they can be sought out in that way, that they survive in captivity.

It's true, as I describe in this book, that if you travel for 27 hours on a bus and at the end find a view from your hotel room of a blue lake with lemon trees and snow capped mountains, then such a moment might follow. And so it might if you drive 500 miles to the north of Scotland to a warm welcome and a cheerful coal fire, but it might not. You could win the lottery, have a grand world tour and never have a single magic moment, or you can be waiting at the reception desk in a garage on Christmas Eve, hear a sentimental Christmas song on the mechanics' radio and there it is.

They come unbidden. They come when you least expect. They come when you give up looking. I've a suspicion though that they are there all the time, but that our anxiety, our self-obsession, our habits, our dependencies prevent us from seeing them, appreciating them.

Despite my earlier reservations about the phrase, I see I've reverted to calling them 'magic moments.' Well it's a handy phrase and conveys the meaning, but there really is nothing magic about such moments. They are reality. They are what life is like, if only we could see. Such a shame that we live all our lives and only glimpse a handful of them, only a dozen or so times do we grasp the truth, the great secret of life: the moment is all there is.

The First Noel

You've got to remember the world was much bigger in those days, four or five times bigger.

I try to visualise it, but there's little of the original memory left. This is a reconstruction, an artist's impression. All I remember is being very small, in the dark, with a spectacle of coloured lights before me. Shadowy figures loom aloft. One of them is Dad. There's snow on the ground. Dad's brought me on my sledge to see the village Christmas tree.

It's December in 1950 or 1951. We're in Queensbury, an industrial village on the Pennine hills between Bradford and Halifax. Until John Foster built Black Dyke Mills in the mid-nineteenth century, there was nothing there but the turnpike road and the Queens Head Inn, a welcome stopping place. It's a climb from whichever direction you arrive.

And fulfilling the prophecy of its name, the mill becomes black. The rows of terraced houses become black. The Fosters prosper and build a castle at Littlemoor. At Christmas they invite their workers in for a drink and a mince-pie. They have them enter at the front and leave at the back. When the benevolent Fosters recognize the same faces coming for seconds, they curtail the enterprise and decline to repeat it. Later the family acquire a real castle at Hornby in Lancashire.

I was born in 1948.

It was as if the smoke from bombed ruins still hung in the air; the echoes of war still reverberated. There was still rationing. There was still a sense of exhaustion. The discomforts of life were never far away. It was grey. It was threadbare. We lived at 35 West End, a house of two rooms - one room downstairs and a bedroom. There was a cellar. The house was a blind-back - no door or windows at the back. There was something that rolled marbles back and forth at night on the stone floor, but it never manifested itself further.

At the front there was a step and the pavement. The step had to be 'donkey-stoned' frequently to show you were house-proud. The milkman's horse, Roger, put his head in the house, hoping for crusts and would bite if they were not forthcoming. There was no toilet in the house. It was round the corner down a side street and shared with half a dozen others. People used to think it was unhygienic to have a toilet in the house. The bath was a tin one, kept in the cellar and put in front of the fire when in use.

But there was dried milk from the clinic and orange juice. There was free health treatment, free dental care, free glasses. The Labour government, swept in after the war, was keeping its promises. This was going to be a land fit for heroes.

Most of my family worked at Black Dyke Mills. Most of the people in the village worked there or had done. Maybe the mill brought out that edge there was in people, or made it keener. Maybe it was the climate. At nearly 1000 feet above sea-level, Queensbury had its own climate. Often it was lost in dank, dripping cloud. Often there was snow, when only rain fell elsewhere. Often there was wind, no always there was wind, a wind that blew all the way from Morecambe.

Queensbury folk were awkward, not uncoordinated, but difficult, cussed. When the Chartists, those early pioneers for improvements in the lives of mill operatives and other working men and women, marched through the village, the workers defended the mill, not out of loyalty to the Fosters, but just to be awkward. They would bear grudges. They would nurture animosities. They would seek out grievances. They were alert for slights. This was particularly prevalent within families. People loved nothing better than the chance to fall out, to not be speaking to their brother, or sister, or father. In an isolated community, before television, there wasn't much else to do. The sour savagery of the bleak moorlands was never far away. It was the spirit Emily Bronte caught in Wuthering Heights. Queensbury was full of dour Josephs, bloody-minded Heathcliffs and shrill Cathys.

Did Christmas bring a truce? Did it bring the spirit of goodwill? Did it bring families together? Not it! No it was an opportunity to twist the knife. It gave a bit of spice to a falling-out. What better than not to invite somebody, not send a card, not buy them owt, not even wish them the compliments of the season. Not that buying presents was much done then, only for your kids, and that often with an eye to outdoing others.

So Christmas was not like it is now. There was not much to buy and not much to buy it with. Nobody had television, but there was the wireless, and there was the cinema with Christmas films like 'Holiday Inn,' 'It's a Wonderful Life,' and 'Scrooge' with Alastair Sim, but the worlds they depicted were a million miles from Queensbury. Well maybe not 'Scrooge.' Ebeneezer would have been welcome in Queensbury, until he went soft.

What was Christmas to me then? I remember nothing of it apart from this night-time sledge ride.

What do I remember?

I can remember playing with sticks of firewood. My mother

used to draw Noddy or Big Ears on them and my father carved them out. I remember the sparks in the soot on the chimney back and how they flew, one by one, up the chimney. I remember a baby's bath on stilts, a yellow rubber affair. How old was I then? I don't know. And how old when my father pulled me along on a sledge to see the village tree? I don't know that either. I guess two or three, because we moved to Bradford when I was four.

What makes it a magic moment? Well in part I know it must have been - being pulled along on a sledge in the dark through the snow to see the wonder of this glowing tree. Of course in my mind I'm seeing it as an observer seeing myself, like Scrooge visiting his past Christmases, and this isn't how it was at the time. Maybe I was cold. Maybe I was overawed. Maybe I was bewildered. Maybe I'm just imagining it, having been told later that that's what happened.

But I believe that even at that age I recognised that this was something special, a vision that showed there was something beyond the narrow post-war, Queensbury existence, something that transcended the mundane.

Those multi-coloured lights stirring in the night wind, with the blue/black snow beyond, were a glimpse of something better, of something more glorious - a bit of magic.

Fee Fi Fo Fum

"I can smell meat!"

Miss Cross's declaration stunned the infant class like a lash of summer lightning.

There were some little tykes there, hard cases, who could not have been abashed by anything less weighty than a boilerman's shovel, but even their grimy faces paled. Think of the horror on my face then; the most sensitive soul in the class, whom a harsh word could bruise. Think of me, who invariably had the meat in question stuffed into the pocket of his short, corduroy pants.

There are lots of issues with food, but when you're a child, the main problem is that you've little control over what you eat. Food gave me more pain than pleasure in my early years. I seemed to be always under pressure to eat things I didn't want to eat, and meat was the worst thing. There were families in Queensbury who'd gnaw a cow down to its shiny bones quicker than locusts. Heels, brains, udder, tripe, tail and tongue, they'd be dispatched with relish, so there were no concessions for finicky kids: meat came red in tooth and claw, with generous attachments of fat and gristle.

It was the elasticity of fat that appalled me; the rubbery quality that meant you were never sure, even when it was swallowed that it would stay swallowed. I judged food by appearances. Cooked onions looked repellently slimy. Currants and raisins looked like flies, or hunched up spiders. Sago pudding looked like frog spawn. I didn't like food with unexpected consistencies. The skin on hot milk made me shudder. Even worse was the skin on rice pudding. Sausages always had gobbets of fat. Bacon was fringed with fat. On the whole I was happier with a treacle sandwich, and by treacle I mean golden syrup. My other staple was a saucer of condensed milk. Mum made rather nice plain, inoffensive buns and an almond cake, but I steered well clear of her Christmas cakes with its generous measures of quasi insects.

Staying to dinner was compulsory at Queensbury Church School: dragging unwilling kids there once a day was considered ordeal enough for mothers, besides most mothers were at work. You have to remember that this was just after the war when there was still rationing and everyone could remember when food was in short supply. There wasn't much sympathy for anyone who refused 'good' food. And I suppose the food was good by today's standards when burger and chips, or just chips, sustain schoolchildren. There'd be meat and two veg; albeit fatty mutton, lumpy mash and stringy cabbage.

Declining it was not an option. If you didn't eat it the dinner ladies would come out and force-feed you, literally. I've seen more than one lad be sick in his sago pudding and often remarked to myself how little changed it seemed by its brief visit to his stomach. I could manage the veg - all I could do with the meat was hide it in my pockets, with the danger that Miss Cross's quivering nose would later detect it.

And detect it she often did. Prowling round the class, half crouching, she might as well have been intoning 'Fee Fi Fo Fum, I smell the blood of an Englishman.' When she pinpointed the culprit, there'd be a perfect storm of hair-pulling, shrieking, and leg slapping, but it was better than having to eat the meat.

Although school dinners was the worst of it, it was generally agreed among adults that I should be eating things I didn't want to. There wasn't a lot of eating done away from home, but at weddings, christenings, funerals, etc aunts and uncles would get indignant about wasted food and my finicky ways. At home, although Dad shared their opinion, he didn't take issue with it often and Mum didn't do at all, if I wanted treacle sandwiches or a saucer of condensed milk, then that's what I got.

When we moved to Bradford the school dinner ordeal ended, Mum and Dad worked shifts, so there was always someone at home at dinner-time. My diet became more varied. Beans on toast became my staple, with tinned mandarin oranges to follow. Meat was on the menu too but in more acceptable forms, eg corned beef, or in stews with dumplings, or pies with suet crusts. It was squeamishness rather than morality that deterred me from eating meat, but then there was a curious aberration.

Encouraged by Dad I became a fan of Tarzan books, saw myself as the 'Lord of the Jungle,' wrestling giant apes, breaking the necks of unruly lions, dropping from the trees on to unsuspecting antelopes, and tearing out haunches of red meat, steaming and dripping with blood. I began to crave raw flesh and persuaded Dad to let me taste some next time he got a joint. The craving didn't survive a tentative taste; the gap between the idea and the reality was insurmountable.

Most of what I ate came out of tins. In addition to beans, there was tomato soup, pea and ham soup, vegetable soup, all accompanied by a stack of sliced white bread. Mum gave up work when Linda was born and thereafter ran a kind of café service, making meals as and when required. Dad was on shifts, so might want his dinner at three in the afternoon, or eleven at night. I'd be home for dinner just after twelve. Sunday was the only meal we had together - Yorkshire puddings, meat and veg.

Fish and chips was a treat, even though it was a cheap meal then: one shilling, or 5p, eight old pence for fish and four for chips. I sometimes used to be indulged and get two fish and no chips. Most of the chip shops were good, but the one in Old Road in Bradford stands out. When I was working in the mill myself, I'd call in after the two till ten shift. I was a battery-filler, keeping the looms supplied with weft, on my feet for eight hours. I'd be tired and grimy with oil, as I waited in the queue for my fish. It certainly sharpened the appetite.

Generally Yorkshire fish and chip shops are better than Lancashire ones. Apart from using beef dripping, they don't diversify like the Lancashire ones, with their curry sauce, jumbo sausages, pies of all kinds, beans and peas. In Yorkshire they concentrate on fish and chips and fishcakes. Harry Ramsden's is often cited, but almost any street corner chippy is OK, preferably with a middle aged couple in charge; him being bald and droll, her being well-rounded and well-organised. The seaside ones are the best, but then you have the sea breeze to sharpen your appetite. What could be better than to be walking along the front at Filey with fish and chips, distant lighthouses in prospect, and bed and a bottle of beer at your digs to look forward to?

I never did much cooking at home. If I got back late at night and if there was nobody up, I'd open a tin and warm up the contents, but if Mum was still up, she'd be on her feet waiting for my order. As a sullen teenager I often had meals in my room and Mum would trail up with them.

Going to college introduced me to a whole new range of foods. I'd never had rice as a savoury before, nor spaghetti, except out of a tin. I shared a flat at Noster Hill in Leeds with Richard Pitt and on Sunday he would prepare Vesta beef curry. There was a packet of rice to boil up and dried curry to mix with water and heat. I thought this was marvellous - real cooking at last. Later when four of us shared at Cranbrook Avenue, Barney made meals from scratch with real vegetables which had to be peeled and cooked. When I met Penny I had spaghetti Bolognese for the first time and lasagne and pizza, and garlic and mince.

Food generally in the early 1970s was getting more varied and exciting. Indian restaurants and Italian restaurants were opening. Fast food was appearing too - Wimpey Bars. I remember a week in London when I had Wimpey-burger and chips every day, sometimes twice a day.

I was not, and still am not, a fan of eating out. It seems to me to be a private activity, and, over 50 years later, there's still fall-out from the trauma of being forced fed as an infant. There's still a slight unease when I'm going to eat somewhere unfamiliar. And, although I've had some pleasant meals out, I don't think I've ever had anything better than even I could do at home for myself, and certainly nothing better than Mum could do.

When our student days, our hippy days were behind us, we children of the sixties took to giving dinner parties to show off, not only our adventurous cuisine, but our Mary Quant, Laura Ashley and Habitat inspired decor. There was a competitive edge to it - who could do the most adventurous dishes, the most authentic ones, but so long as there was plenty wine flowing I didn't mind. In the end though the food seemed to get in the way of a pleasant evening's drinking.

Today more than ever food's beset with ethical problems. If you can buy a coconut in Tesco for 50p, what's the person who grew it getting paid? Food's too cheap and there's too much choice. I once counted seventeen varieties of vinegar in Sainsburys. What would a nineteenth century mill worker make of a modern supermarket? And then there's battery farming, salmon farming, genetically modified crops, the use of pesticides, the huge subsidies to European farmers. There's obesity and other health problems. There's the vegetarian issue - surely in the 21st century we should have progressed beyond using our fellow inhabitants of the planet for food. Food's always been a political and moral issue, from the potato famine and corn laws, back to the days when peasants were hanged for poaching. Food's a problem.

I've come a long way since the days when beans on toast was my staple diet - now I have Lancashire cheese and mustard on the toast and top the beans with an egg, or two.

Over the Rainbow

Walking was a major recreation for us in Queensbury in the post-war years, not hiking, not rambling. There was no special equipment, no boots, no waterproofs - Goretex hadn't been invented. There were no maps. Often we set off on a Sunday morning while Mum was making dinner, lunch as it would be now, sometimes on a Sunday afternoon, when Mum would go too.

In those days the countryside flowed into semi-urban areas like Queensbury. There was a network of ginnels and snickets that would lead to fields, without the need to cross roads or streets. Like wormholes in space they'd take you from the High St, with its buses and lorries, and horses and carts, to a field full of buttercups and cows. Some ginnels had iron bollards at the entrance and well-worn flags, others were more furtive, merely gaps, margins, left-over scraps, but faithful to ancient footways.

There would be expeditions to Shibden Valley, which, in season, might involve bilberrying or blackberrying. Sometimes we would go as far as Ogden Moors, and have to catch a bus to Causeway Foot. Sometimes we would go 'window-shopping' to Bradford or Halifax.

Sometimes the walks were no more than a perambulation of the village to call at aunties or Joe Glover's sweet shop. There were three aunties: Auntie Carrie, Auntie Maria, and Auntie Elsie - Dad's sisters. Auntie Carrie was only just round the corner, out of sight, but not always out of earshot. She was a big woman, over sixteen stone, with a face as expressive and guileless as a young child, with small black eyes like currants in dough. Her husband Jim was practically deaf. Her youngest son Ronnie had Downs Syndrome. He was fond of David Whitfield and played his records at full blast. Her eldest, Stuart, was mean and lean, with greased-back, black hair. He wore black leather jackets and rode a motorbike - one of Queensbury's first rockers. They all communicated at the tops of their voices. They had perfected the 'wall of sound,' before Phil Spector had even got into the record business.

Auntie Maria lived in Cardigan Street down Sandbeds. She was small, dark and shrewd, with glittering eyes. She had four sons: Peter, David, Jackie and Philip. I only remember Philip and Jackie; Peter and David were much older and had left home. They both ended up in North America. Philip was about my own age, Jackie was older, dead-pan and droll, with something of the teddy boy, but more of the teddy bear him. Her husband, my uncle Herbert had a 40 Woodbines a day voice and would be in the Ring o' Bells, or the Stag's Head, or waiting outside for one of them to open.

Maria had a smoky voice. My Dad smoked. Jackie did too. They had a budgie. The room would be marbled with smoke: skeins of fresh blue smoke and drifting banks of hazy grey smoke from previous cigarettes. The budgie smoked too, albeit involuntarily.

Auntie Elsie's was different - no smoke, no children, husband at home - Harold, a pint-sized Harry Secombe. Elsie was snowy-haired, like a dandelion that had clocked, as Dad said once when she'd had it permed. Her smile reached all the way to her blue eyes. She was less challenging than Carrie or Maria. The chimney breast in their front room boasted a piece of Harold's craft-work: a view of a lane disappearing over a hill, with decorative trees. It was brown and cream and done in marquetry.

There was another 'Uncle Harold,' Harold Sutcliffe, no relation and so different - skinny, feckless, mischievous, with a dash of ... well, dash. He was a mate of Dad's. They'd got to know each other on the bus to work. Coincidentally Mum had got to know his wife Audrey, taking me to the clinic. Audrey's daughter Gillian was about my age. She had another daughter, Shirley who was older.

Harold's insouciance attracted and irritated Dad. 'If he fell of t' Co-op, he'd fall into t'divi,' was his frequent prediction. In fact Harold's life was not particularly charmed and he died at the young age of 52. Dad referred to him as 'Sutcliffe,' a term of affectionate derision, and Sutcliffe he will be throughout this book. Things happened when he was around; he couldn't walk 100 yards down the path without having an adventure. To me he was always the harbinger of good times and I remember him fondly.

None of the aunts or uncles did any walking, nor did most folk. The countryside may not have been the desolate place it once had seemed to be, before the romantic movement opened people's eyes to the beauty of nature. Most folk were prepared to concede its attractions, but wanted to be taken there in a bus.

Shibden is a corruption of sheep dean, meaning sheep valley. It was a lost world, a left-over from an inter-glacial period when there were lush forests and dense vegetation and streams of bright water. At its head were quarries, with heather amid the emerald grass. At the bottom were historic halls: Scout Hall built in the mid seventeenth century by John Mitchell, with its bas relief sculpture over the front door of a hunting scene; Upper Shibden Hall, where in 1634 Sir Thomas Browne set up his first practice and wrote 'De Religio Medici,' and the timber framed Shibden Hall, built in 1420 by the Otes family.

We only had to walk down Deanstones Lane and climb a stile and we were in Shibden Valley. This was better than any municipal park or playground. Here there were quarries to scale, trees to climb, steep valley sides to swarm up, streams to run down - leaping from one slippery boulder to the next. There was a wall with a tunnel running through it, which Dad called the Roman wall.

Lower down was a disused brewery, masked by the trees, as though hiding from the revenue men. A nearby stream was milky and stinking. Sometime we walked this way and emerged at Ambler Thorn and made a round trip of it. Once on a hot day, when I was all aglow, weary, sweaty and thirsty, Dad bought me an ice lolly at the little shop at the bottom of Roper Lane. It was grapefruit and I remember it to this day. How intense an experience it must have been. The only other ice lolly I remember nearly as well was a blue mint one bought from the van that used to park by Cooper Lane School. They cost a penny and were frozen in little aluminium tubes.

'Window shopping,' which we did back in the 1950s, would be hard to do now - the shops are open on Sundays. We'd catch the bus into Bradford or Halifax and wander round the shops, inspecting the window displays and imagining what we would buy if the shop had been open and we'd had the money. It wasn't a favourite activity of mine, but Dad enjoyed it, secure in the knowledge that he wasn't going to have to put his hand in his pocket.

For most, walking was not an end then, but a means. You walked because you had no car, and saving the bus-fare was significant - you'd be in Joe Glover's a long time, scanning his jars of boiled sweets and toffees spending a two penny bus-fare. People would undertake walks that would seem daunting today. Dad sometimes trekked the seven or eight miles to work in Shipley when there was no bus. Grandad trailed the four or five miles from Manningham

Lane on Christmas Day when there was no bus.

And yet walking for me was fun; walking over Ogden Moor to the Buttresses was an exhilarating experience - flying with your feet on the ground. And when you got to Fly Flatts by the Withens pub, there were lost horizons; to the west; to the south; to the north. There were footpaths racing away in every directions: stony tracks that curved invitingly out of sight.

And this is it, this is the point that we come to at last, and I don't know on what particular occasion it stirred in me, but I saw once a snicket, or a lane, or a footpath curving away, its direction perhaps masked by trees in full leaf, and it spoke to me of mystery and adventure, of discovery, of new worlds, of something beyond words, of something just, beyond...

And still today I can see it, a bend in the lane, a certain turn in the way ahead, or a side-road, and my heart thus quickens - the world beyond the rainbow beckons.

Beside the Sea

Despite the claim chalked up on the blackboard leaning against the radiator grille, it was not a magical mystery tour. The orange and cream Westercroft coach parked up by the war memorial on sunny summer Sundays was going to Temple Newsham. Everybody knew that.

There were other excursions too: to Morecambe, Blackpool, New Brighton, Bridlington, and Scarborough. From Bradford, Wallace Arnold coaches went even further afield, and from Chester Street bus station, the big red Bristols and Leylands of the West Yorkshire Service ran to destinations all over the Dales. Buses were big in the 1950s. Buses got you to where you wanted to go.

I can remember the excitement of climbing aboard. I can remember the feel of the plush upholstery against my bare legs. I can remember the anxiety lest the bus go before everybody got on, an anxiety born and exacerbated by Sutcliffe's habit of always being late, and, at the half-way pub stop, of always having a last pint, when there wasn't time, and having to run across the coach-park. He would be impervious though to the indignant glares of the other passengers when he boarded at last.

I can still feel an echo of the excitement to this day when I board a bus and settle down in my seat. And yet when the moment came I'm not sure whether I was on the bus, or on the train.

The annual holidays for Bradford were in August, at Bowling Tide, Halifax's were in July. We would leave the house early in the morning, like moonlight-flitters. The light would be a sickly hue. I would be sitting on a suitcase by the door, full of dismay at having been parted from my warm bed and my dreams, and full of apprehension at all this stealthy activity.

A last check round - are all the windows locked? Is everything switched off, turned off? Then we would be out on the damp street. August or not, fine or not, there would be a chill in the air at this time in the morning. Dad would try the door, put away his keys, take a suitcase in each hand, get his balance and then we'd be off down the road to the bus terminus.

Bradford's Exchange Station was a rather grander affair than its present incarnation. The glass roof vaulted aloft, the concourse thronged with travellers and porters wheeling luggage. The stalls were half way to becoming exotic bazaars. The toilets and the bar such as you might find in foreign parts. You'd have to be at a major airport today to get the feel of it - major seaport it seemed like then, with great steamers berthed, waiting for embarkation.

These massive smoke-wreathed engines caught their breath, panted, hissed, and exhaled clouds of steam. They were distant cousins to the earth-bound mill engines familiar to many of the queuing passengers. They terrified me. They must indeed have seemed as vast as ocean liners, getting up steam. Doors were slammed. Whistles were blown. Steam was let off. Couplings would lurch and jar. Iron wheels would begin to roll, begin to hammer a slow rhythm over the iron rails. The acoustics would change as we emerged from under the canopy of the station, become quieter, but by then I would be in tears.

We'd be heading for Scarborough. The grimy stone of Bradford would give way to the grimy red brick of Leeds and then fields would supervene. Telegraph wires would dip and lift, dip and lift. The carriages would sway. The wheels would fly, singing, rapping along the rails. They were compartment trains then, with pictures, seaside views, over the seats. There was always the sound of doors being slid apart - Sutcliffe on his way to the bar.

I would fall asleep, and when I awoke, would be reconciled to this new world, this unfamiliar, unpredictable world. Whither were we heading? Was it from here that I first saw it? Was it from the carriage window that I first got my glimpse of it, or was it from the bus, that I first saw the sea? That dramatic transformation, that sudden ending of the world as I'd always known it, and its continuation as a blue, glittering expanse that ruled a straight line against the distant sky.

I can't remember the moment, the original moment, but the ripples of my astonishment can still be felt today whenever I approach the coast, or turn a corner in a seaside town and see it there at the end of the street: that beautiful, alien, mysterious entity that now whispers, now roars, now lies as still as marbled glass, now surges and seethes, that medium that reflects the sky, now blue, now grey, now white - the sea.

Mrs Young's boarding house in Castle Road, Scarborough, had been our holiday destination for longer than I could remember. My parents had been going there since they were married in 1944. She ran a clean, welcoming establishment and was a good cook. Her Yorkshire puddings put Mum's to shame. Dad would glare at her over his well-risen plateful, as though to say, 'this is what they're supposed to be like.'

Alas Mrs Young got old. It all got too much for her. We were sitting there one lunchtime, knives and forks at the ready like members of the 'Beano Sausage and Mash Club,' when from the bay window we could see her leaving with her shopping bag. Lunch was late that day.

We patronised another establishment for a while run by the dashing Claud Scullion, the finest swordsman in the whole of Scarborough, who had taken part in one of the last cavalry charges of the British Army in the First World War. He had a wonderful collection of swords, many of them supplied to him by bin-men. One generation's rubbish is a later one's treasure.

At boarding houses then you had to be out by nine and were not allowed back till noon. After dinner you had to stay away again till teatime. It was now that the stamina built up on our Sunday walks paid dividends. It was a rare day when you could sit on the beach for more than an hour. If it wasn't raining the North Sea wind would whip the sand up into a blizzard and send unoccupied deck chairs scudding along.

Window shopping skills were not redundant either, as we walked round and round the shops until the displays were imprinted on our memories. Sometimes we'd walk up to the castle. Sometimes we'd walk along Marine Drive to the North Bay. We'd walk and we'd walk. I would drag my spade along behind me, both of us whining tinnily. We'd walk until my feet were hot, my head swimming and my legs like jelly, then Dad would hoist me on to his shoulders and I'd be up there among the seagulls, lolling wearily, lulled by Brylcream fumes.

In the evening there'd be Peaseholm Park and the magic of the illuminated 'Tree Walk.' And then back at to the digs at last for the night - me with my comics - 'Classics Illustrated,' I remember, but that must have been when I was older, Mum with her magazine, and Dad with his westerns and a bottle of rum, which he kept locked in his suitcase. It would be a cosy hour amid the bleak austerity of the boarding house regime.

And then time to go home. By now though Scarborough was my home. It had imprinted itself upon me, with its beach and sea and amusement arcades and funfair and shops. I didn't want to go. The idea made me feel faint and made my heart race with panic. I was in tears all the way back, couldn't get a last look at the sea because of them. Not sure about Mum, but suspect she was less than thrilled at the prospect of returning to grim, post-war Queensbury. Dad would have been more stoical.

The neighbours were pleased to see us though. When Dad had turned off the water at the stopcock in the cellar, he'd turned off the supply to the rest of the row.

Are You Sitting Comfortably?

Early televisions were pieces of furniture, often they had doors, as though there were something not quite proper about them, like commodes. Now of course lounges flaunt their huge, flat screens. We had a television as early as 1952, while we were still living in Queensbury. Viewing was done in the dark, with the curtains drawn. This was to improve picture quality, but also echoed the cinema and added a bit of drama.

And yet it's the radio that I remember best from those days. Our set was encased in polished walnut veneer and sat on the sideboard. Dad said it was full of tiny people who did all the programmes and for a long time I believed him and would peer through the ventilation holes at the back and glimpse the city of glowing valves trying to spot its diminutive citizens.

I remember 'Listen with Mother.'

'The time is a quarter to two. This is the BBC Light Programme for mothers and children at home. Are you ready for the music? When it stops, Catherine Edwards will be here to speak to you. Ding-de-dong. Ding-de-dong, Ding, Ding! Are you sitting comfortably? Then I'll begin!'

I remember listening on summer days when the door stood open and the sounds and scents of the sunny, dusty road wafted in, ineffably enhanced by the gentle voice and music. There was nobody like Catherine Edwards in Queensbury, no soft accents, nothing gentle. I suppose here were seeds of yearning sown. Nobody like Catherine Edwards at Queensbury Church School either.

On Sunday there was the 'Billy Cotton Band Show' on the wireless, always associated with the smells of roast beef. On other days there was 'Archie Andrews,' 'Dick Barton,' 'Workers' Playtime,' 'Mrs Dale's Diary,' 'The Archers.' There were the precise, calm voices of the announcers, voices that had sustained people throughout the War. Radio programmes were right here, inside your head; television was over there on the box in the corner of the room.

But TV prevailed and it was 'Watch With Mother' that became the high spot of the afternoon.' Picture Book' was a reasonable TV adaptation of how 'Listen with Mother' had seemed, and Patricia Driscoll was just the kind of angelic person I had imagined. Andy Pandy was incomprehensible. What was Andy Pandy? What kind of creature was he? I felt uncomfortable about his relationship with Loobyloo. Teddy was OK. Teddy was reassuring. 'Bill and Ben' was best. I liked the farm and the barn and the garden. They were places you could imagine exploring. There was a whole world beyond Bill and Ben and the flowerpots. What was the gardeners cottage like, and his wife, and the village where they went to shop, and the country lanes? I always thought the sea could not be far away. 'Rag Tag and Bobtail' too had a sense of being somewhere - a real wild wood. 'The Woodentops' was too contrived.

There was merchandise even then. I didn't have Bill and Ben models, but I did have Hank and Silver King, characters in 'Whirligig,' shown on Saturday afternoons. Also I had a die-cast Muffin the Mule puppet that clunked around very much as the TV original with Annette Mills.

Mary Malcolm, Sylvia Peters, Macdonald Hobley were programme announcers. They became like glamorous family members. Everyone knew them. They were discussed with Sutcliffe and Audrey and sly allusions were made as to warm feelings existing, protest being belied by blushes. Sutcliffe, as might be expected, managed to get ITV before it was supposed to be broadcast in the north. How exciting it was to see the first adverts. I remember the toothpaste ones - Pepsodent - 'wonder where the yellow went,' and Gibbs SR. There was something flashy and trashy about ITV. I felt it at the time, compelling as many of their programmes were.

Getting a good picture was always a performance. Down in Bradford our TV aerial was in the attic, so Mum would be in the front room, I would be on the landing and Dad in the attic moving the aerial about.

"It's better."

"It's worse."

"That's it."

"No it's worse than ever."

Tempers were easily lost. Dad would descend and glare at the set.

"I thought you said it was a good picture."

"Well it was when I said."

"Well it isn't now."

"Oh, what does it matter? It's all rubbish anyway." Mum would say, undermining the whole business, as she so often did.

Television became part of my life. It would be on as soon as I got home from school. I'd do my homework watching 'Robin Hood,' or 'Ivanhoe,' or 'William Tell,' or 'Sir Lancelot.' I would watch adult programmes too, watch anything apart from sport. We didn't watch a lot of sport, though Dad liked the wrestling, which Mum loathed. Mum liked Tony Hancock, but Dad sneered at him. Mum was a BBC person and Dad more of an ITV one. Their tastes coincided sometimes: they both hated 'Coronation Street.' They both liked 'The Black and White Minstrels.' They went for personalities: Gilbert Harding, Fanny Cradock, Ken Dodd; others - Hughie Green, Bruce Forsyth, Michael Miles were too 'full of themselves.' They preferred people with a touch of vulnerability.

American TV was slicker, pacier, more glamorous. There were comedies - 'Lucille Ball,' 'I Married Joan,' 'Phil Silvers;' dramas - 'Dr Kildare,' and 'Highway Patrol;' and, of course, westerns - 'Wagon Train,' 'Cheyenne,' 'Maverick.' And then in the sixties British TV blossomed. Along came 'Steptoe,' 'The Likely Lads,' ' Till Death us do Part,' 'The Wednesday Play', 'Play for Today,' 'TW3,' 'Not So Much a Programme.'

Of course it helped that 'Ready Steady Go,' and 'Top of the Pops' could feature The Rolling Stones, and The Beatles, who were changing the world of pop music, changing the world of teenage fashion, changing the world. Both bands appeared on 'Sunday Night at the London Palladium' too, The Stones, enhancing their bad boy image by refusing to appear on the revolving stage at the end. The Beatles were still in the light entertainment tradition and were happy to send themselves up, making films like 'A Hard Day's Night,' and 'Help.'

It helped too that TV could show England winning the World Cup in 1966, watched by 33 million viewers in the UK alone. TV in the 1960s unified the nation. There were only two channels. Everybody saw 'Cathy Come Home,' and was talking about it next day. Everybody watched 'Z Cars,' and 'Dr Who,' and 'Adam Adamant,' and 'The Forsyte Saga.' Maybe TV had too much power then, maybe it's better now that it's lost its hold, become fragmented, can no longer command a universal audience. As they say there's nothing to stay in for on a Saturday night now.

TV had no part to play in my days as a student. Later, in both married lives I became addicted to certain programmes. I got quite emotional about some of them. The signature tunes of 'Cheers,' 'Golden Girls,' 'Auf Wiedersehen Pet,' and 'Only Fools and Horses,' almost brought tears to my eyes.

When we went on holiday to a caravan or cottage, the first thing I did was make sure the TV was working, and often it wasn't, particularly in the Highlands. Disaster - I'd miss the latest about Del and Rodney. I got homesick for Peckham. It was escapism. Later when I had escaped, I'd no need of it. I stopped watching TV. I knew I was missing some good programmes, but for me it had lost its power.

It Isn't Very Good in the Dark, Dark Wood...

It's almost 50 years since I ran through the evening Woods as fleet as a deer - the exhilaration, the exaltation of the moment are with me today. I was boundless. I was Mercury. I was airborne. I could have run for ever.

Oh what a poor thing my body is now. How the 50 years weigh on me like the fathoms of forged iron that encumbered Jacob Marley. Oh my worn joints. Oh my flaccid muscles. Oh my 101 aches and pains. Oh the nausea of a 1001 years of excess. If the poor boy of ten could swap for a moment and squeeze into this doleful ruin, how he would howl with dismay and think the hour of his death was nigh, and count it a blessing.

And what of me? What if I could swap and feel how it was then, how it was to be a ten year old with a body as light as thistle down and as lithe as a willow wand, a body whose every cell was pink and pollution free and whose every atom was replaced long before its sell- by-date? Oh the bliss. Oh the joy. I would float. Gravity would have no purchase on me.

The Woods were behind Windermere Road. There are houses there now. Where once troops of skinny Tarzans swung through the trees, are now centrally heated bedrooms with fitted wardrobes and en suite bathrooms, and where once were dens in the undergrowth are now through lounges with patio doors and decking.

It wasn't in truth much of a wood - maybe 100 trees in a few 100 square yards of steep meadow. It was our imaginations that made its depths impenetrable and stretched it to forest clad horizons. My first memory of it is of being alone there on a November night, guardian of the bonfire, expected to protect it from the dreaded 'Jer Street Gang.' I could only have been five or six.

I was more of a goat than a guard, a goat tethered to tempt a stalking tiger into the hunters' sights. I was a newcomer to the 'Windermere Road Gang' and much younger than they. I was expendable. I can feel the sense of alienation to this day. The 'Windermere Road Gang' were softies: Bradford Grammar School Boys, not toughs like the Jer Street lot, who went to Cross Lane Secondary Modern, if they went to school at all.

Alienation was my lot at Cooper Lane School too. At playtime I stood on the steps by the entrance, not daring to venture further. I had it in my mind that there was a dragon at the back of the school chasing the kids, which is why they were forever running back and forth screaming. The alienation persisted until the day I had a fight with Christopher Kellett. It ended inconclusively and afterwards we became friends.

We played in Orford's fields. We played in the Stone Yard where the council stored gravel, salt and sand for the road. We played in the Woods. One reason why kids don't play out so much now, apart from the traffic and fear of paedophiles, is that there's nowhere to play.

In the event the 'Jer Street Gang' did not put in an appearance and the bonfire survived to smudge the foggy November the fifth night with orange. There were so many fires then. Every street had one. It was an exciting time. The sweet shop opposite the White Horse in Great Horton Road sold fireworks. Two ladies ran it. They put on quite a display in their glass-fronted counter - snowstorms, roman candles, air bombs, rip-raps, their various shapes and packaging as tempting as the adjacent sweets, which were perhaps too adjacent. On the morning of the sixth the air would be heavy with smoke, the fires would still smoulder and we'd collect rocket sticks on the way to school.

The gas-lit street corners of autumn and winter had an excitement all their own. It was made up of the encroaching darkness and the unknown, and of the creepy tales we would tell of white things seen flitting in the grave yards and Spring-heeled Jack, who could jump over houses, and the thing that was sometimes seen in Old Road, a bear-like thing, raising its arms on high and prostrating itself like a worshipper. But spring and summer were the seasons for playing out.

What did we play? Well formal games such as cricket, never football, and hide and seek and British Bulldog, if there were enough of us, but the games of the imagination were best, games of valour and glorious death. Back in the 1950s we were still fighting the Germans. The comics, 'Wizard,' 'Rover,' 'The Dandy' and 'The Beano' all featured stories in which the Germans shouted 'Kamerad' and 'Mein Gott,' and threw down their weapons as they surrendered to steel-jawed Tommies. Our fathers and our grandfathers had fought the Germans and we were fighting them still.

The Wehrmacht never did invade and penetrate as far as Orford's Fields, or the Stone Yard, or the Woods, but in our games they did and we gave them the shock of their lives. Panzer Divisions, battle-hardened on the Eastern front, didn't expect to encounter the ferocity and bravado of small boys with toy guns.

I had quite an arsenal of toy guns: double-barrelled pop guns that fired corks, revolvers that fired caps. I got a pair of those, as used by the Cisco Kid, just before I went into hospital; scant consolation. I got a Winchester rifle once, a disappointment. It advertised itself as ejecting bullets, which I took to mean shooting them, but it didn't, it meant what it said - ejecting, as in ejecting spent cartridge cases. I also had a plastic Thompson machine gun that the Germans learned to fear with good cause.

When I ran through the Woods on that evening though we were not giving Gerry a bloody nose. On the strength of my Scarborough holidays with the ex-cavalryman Major Scullion, and his having shown me a few passes with a sabre, I decided I was Claude Duvalle, the finest swordsman in Standard Four at Horton Bank Top Junior School. My sword was a garden cane with the plastic lid off my sister's toy teapot, drilled through to make a hilt. I was running through the Woods with my sword pushed through my snake belt.

Before Windermere Road, Hollybank Road, and Great Horton Road were built, there'd have been nothing but swooping, green fields from Old Road right down to Clayton, green fields and trees. The Woods were all that was left.

It was a summer evening and there was that fresh, benign quality in the air, partly smelled, partly felt. I was running along the path through the trees, running lightly, running well within myself. And then suddenly I knew how strong and light and indefatigable I was. I ran on for sheer joy. I ran and ran and felt I could have kicked off the world, kicked it away behind me like an old football and surged into the constellations, breasting the stars, scattering them in my wide-eyed glee

Under the Christmas Tree

I was standing in the multi-hued penumbra of the Christmas tree, in the bay-window watching for the bus. It had been snowing. The main road and pavement were white over. You couldn't tell where one began and the other ended. Cars were having trouble getting up the 'Bank.'

We moved when I was five and what a contrast. From the 'one up one down' in Queensbury, to a large Victorian villa on Great Horton Road in Bradford. It had three bedrooms, two attic bedrooms, four cellar rooms, a dumb waiter, a balcony, a verandah, a stained glass window of Hamlet gazing at Yorick's skull, a front garden and a back yard. It was Dad's grand, reckless, romantic gesture. His family were in part astonished and in part aghast at his folly. They wandered round it like visitors to a stately home, determined not to be impressed. I don't think their 'you must be crackers,' comments bothered him. I think he knew that underneath they were envious - that such feats of the imagination were beyond them.

Of course buying a house then was not the ruinous racket it is today. He paid about £1000 for it at a time when he was earning about that a year. To buy the same house today would cost you £180,000. He had a good job - weaving overlooker, highly skilled manual work, but I don't think he'd be on £180, 000 a year if he was working today.

I remember the first night there. We all slept in the same bedroom, all except Rufty, the cat. Rufty wasn't out there on his own for long. He came flying at our door, spitting and yowling in terror. We let him in and he spent the night grumbling and staring in horror at the door. Despite that I didn't find the house too scary, only the back attic which I wouldn't go in at any price, not even in the daytime. Oh and there was the time the door of the built-in cupboard in my bedroom opened and the old man with the white beard looked out. I did a fair imitation of Rufty myself, hurling myself at the door of Mum and Dad's room. It was probably just a dream.

Victoriana was not prized in the 1950s, in fact it was regarded as dated and ugly. Out came Hamlet, to be replaced with frosted glass, out came the dumb waiter, all the ornate fireplaces went, replaced by modern tiled ones. The panelled doors were covered with hardboard, as were the fancy bannisters. Bright colours were the thing, stripey, starry wallpapers with borders, jazzy curtains, formica tops - everything had to be gay and clean and simple, modern and brilliant.

Even after Dad had finished with it, it was still a house made for Christmas. Christmas is a Victorian invention. The house was Victorian and when that good old time of the year came round, it was in its element. Dad was too. He had a huge appetite for the season. In those days Christmas goods were not in the shops in September like now, but Dad would get the Drivers and the Dyson and Horsfall's Christmas catalogues, forerunners of today's mail-order catalogues, and would be making selections and lists.

There were artificial trees then as now, an American toilet brush company had been making them, since before the War, but they were not convincing then, nor now, and anybody who had one didn't understand the true spirit of Christmas.

Dad brought home real trees, trees such as might have done a village square proud. And, big as the front room was, high as the ceiling was, he would always have to saw a foot or two off the bottom, to stop the top bending over against the ceiling. And the lights! What lights we had! Each one was a little ornament in its own right. Some were shaped like lanterns: square lanterns, spherical lanterns, cylindrical lanterns; some were figurines: St Nicholas, angels, snowmen; and some were animals and birds, reindeer and parrots. They were from eastern Europe. Dad got them from a Ukrainian at work. They were glass, but solid, coloured glass, weighty things, and they looked good even before they were switched on, and when they were, when they were arranged at last and switched on - how they glowed. I've never seen the like of them since. We used them even when they no longer worked and had been usurped by ordinary, pear-shaped coloured lights. Later we got 'bubble-lights,' which had glass tubes full of coloured liquid that bubbled when they got warm.

But the tree was only part of it. In those days when you trimmed up for Christmas, you really trimmed up. As early as the end of November I'd have packs of crepe paper from Woolworths: red, green, lemon, blue, white, and in the evenings I'd cut them into strips to make paper chains. It wouldn't be long before I was glued up, with the paper links sticking to my fingers. Mum made roses out of crepe paper: red, yellow and white roses, with green leaves and a stem. I thought they were wonderful. She used to make a fancy crepe paper bow to tie round the bucket the tree stood in.

There were bought trimmings too; ones made out of coloured tissue paper. They came flat, with cardboard at each end. They opened out, opened out far enough to cross the room from corner to corner. They came in oblongs, squares, circles, polygons. There was a red string running through the middle to support the weight. Both downstairs rooms and the hallway were festooned; from the corners to the light-fittings and then along the walls from corner to corner. There were globes and bells of tissue paper too, again coming flat with protective cardboard covers. These could be opened out fully and suspended from the ceiling, or opened half way and pinned to the wall. When all was done the rustle of paper in the draft was deafening. There were balloons. I could never blow them up, still can't, but Dad would snap them a couple of times and then put them to his lips and blow. They would balloon then alright, even the long, spirally ones. They went in groups in the corners by the ceiling.

And the food - Christmas then really was the only opportunity in the year to indulge. Now you can eat more than is good for you every day of the week, but then only at Christmas would there be chicken and roast potatoes and sausages and sprouts and stuffing and apple sauce. Only then would there be Christmas pudding, Christmas cake, mince pies, fruit, chocolates, and nuts; walnuts, which Dad could crack in his hands, Brazil nuts which he could crack in his teeth, and almonds, which resisted everything but the nut crackers.

Only at Christmas would there be whisky, sherry, brandy, port, advocaat. People didn't drink wine in those days, at least not our kind of people. Chicken's a cheap, every day meal now, but then it was a Christmas treat. Turkeys were eaten too. Of course Dad always bought the biggest. One year the turkey was too big for the oven. He rigged up a spit in front of the fire in the basement and cooked it there. God knows what time he was up in the morning that Christmas, most years he was up at 6.00.

Dad was fond of company, always liked a house-full. Mum didn't. It was a source of endless arguments. On Christmas Day there was a succession of callers: neighbours, relatives, workmates. Dad would ply Walter from the mill with 'Johnnie Walker Black Label' until he was slipping me and my sister half-crowns. Some folk just came to see what we'd got for Christmas and turn their noses up. My Granddad Lorenzo, Mum's Dad, came. He walked from Manningham Lane and back. He used to buy presents for us from the open air market in Bradford - comic books with weird, nightmarish cartoon characters, indoor fireworks, and magic colouring books. He always got a bottle of QC sherry and a box of Mannikin cigars in return.

And so to the moment - standing in the window in the glow of the tree. I was waiting to see Sutcliffe and Audrey and Gillian arrive. The bus from Queensbury was number 53, but the snow had fleeced over the front of the buses and I couldn't read the numbers. In such treacherous conditions, they were all descending the Bank with great care, and they all looked as thought they were stopping, but none did.

Supposing they weren't coming! If the weather was bad here, what would it be like in Queensbury, land of eternal snow? There were no phones then to let people know what was happening, but it wasn't like Sutcliffe to be daunted by a bit of snow.

And so the moment came - Christmas Eve, the room behind me in darkness, but for the fire, not a real one alas, but electric with flickering log effect. The lights on the tree that towered above me were all aglow. Beyond the window, with its reflection of the coloured lights and my dark anxious face, was the rapidly darkening December afternoon and the flying snow. And then came the moment of enlightenment, the lifting of the veil, the suspension of self-awareness, whatever it was - the moment. I was in the moment.

A bus emerged from the darkness like an Ice Age mammoth. Was it just slowing like all the others? No this one was stopping. Not slowing half enough however. Realising this, the driver braked harder and the bus did a little shimmy before it came to a halt, nudging into the bus stop itself.

Three got off. It was them! Before running to announce the news in the kitchen. I lingered to see if there was any more drama. The conductor and driver stood out in the snow looking up at the body of the bus. Sutcliffe exchanged a joke with them and headed for the house, his face wreathed with a grin, his arms full of parcels. It was the way he would have wanted to arrive. Audrey and Gillian floundered in his wake, as best they could.

Dream Homes

More than bricks and mortar; they are the stuff of dreams, dreams of a better life, dreams of lost idylls. They are part of the landscape, part of the area's history. They transcend space and time. These Elizabethan farmhouses with their mullioned windows; these gentleman's houses in Dales villages; these rambling cottages with secret gardens, these are dream homes. If it's possible to live happily ever afterwards, then these are the homes where it could be done.

Are people not ill in such homes? Does nobody ever have a broken heart there? Does nobody die there? They do, of course they do, and have done for generations, but the ancient walls and low-beamed ceilings offer a balm; the beauty soothes; the shared experience of many generations offers consolation

I've described my first childhood house in another piece. It wasn't much different to anyone else's house, though I was enchanted to find there were houses that had back doors, houses you could walk right through. Ours, and most others, were dead ends, a blankness. What lay beyond was a mystery as deep as death to my infant awareness. What a revelation to enter a house in one way and come out somewhere completely different - it was magic.

Mill owners built warehouses for their raw materials, warehouses for their finished goods, warehouses for their workers and country seats in parkland for themselves. When a Lancashire operative complained that the houses were not fit to live in, the mill owner replied. 'They're not for living in, they're for sleeping in: t'mill's for living in.' There were exceptions; Sir Titus Salt and Robert Own built model housing for their workers at Saltaire and New Lanark, and there was the Quaker inspired 'Spring Vale Garden Village' scheme in Darwen, but for the most part houses in the industrial towns were minimal, mean and ugly.

Maybe it was Dad's bold move to 930 Great Horton Road that implanted in my head the idea of a home as an adventure. It was not a beautiful house; a late Victorian terraced villa, built for a manager or senior clerk, but to a four year old it was a soaring, rambling, scary playground. Imagine having a balcony, so lofty that its stone embellishments snagged on the clouds, or a verandah that you could climb up to by getting on the roof of the midden. No ordinary house was ever going to match 930 and the next house we lived in: 23 Windermere Terrace, was very ordinary - a pre-war, pebble-dashed, quasi-semi. We moved because 930 was hard to maintain, expensive to decorate, hard to keep warm and had roof problems that were never really sorted. There was often a network of oilcloth channels tied to the beams to lead leaks to buckets.

The move to 23 Windermere Terrace coincided with the start of my teenage years; shades of the prison-house began to close around me. My bedroom was at the back and I can close my eyes and be there still, though it's 40 years since I was. All the agonies and ecstasies of adolescence took place in that room. I wake even now and for a second fear I'm there.

There was a shed and for the first time we had a garden. We had a lawn and I would put up the tent there and me and Christopher Kellett would sleep out and have perambulations around the streets of Great Horton, Thornton and Clayton, talking, making plans, having daydreams at the dead of night.

It was during my teenage years that I first imagined, and then drew plans, of my ideal house. I've worked on it since, but it was a stone-built, detached house with big bay windows on either side of an imposing entrance. There was a hall with stairs facing, and doors off to sitting room, dining room, library and snooker room. The library had french windows to a walled garden. There was a kitchen, a pantry, and a utility room. There was a cellar of indeterminate extent. There were four bedrooms on the first floor, four further attic ones. There were stables and garages and hen-huts. The river was not far away. It was isolated. It stood at right angles to the road.

I remained at 23 Windermere Terrace until I left home altogether in 1968 and then came a succession of rooms in Beeston in south Leeds - student houses in Noster Hill, Cranbrook Avenue and Tempest Road, all alike in their dreariness and discomfort. Their hearts had died and gone to dust years before. They were anonymous, like hostels, like lodging houses.

Moving from job to job around the country was much easier for public sector workers back in the 1960s and 70s. Most authorities held property vacant for incoming teachers, police, and other staff. On our first day at Blackburn Library, my wife Penny and I got the keys to a flat in a high-rise development. We were on the eleventh floor of Ewood Court, one of three tower blocks at Mill Hill. It was warehouse housing again, but the lounge had windows on two walls, which I've always liked. You came down the dark passage-way and opened the door to airy brightness. And there were views: views of the canal and Billinge Hill and the Royal Infirmary, but it was noisy: you could hear the flats above and below, and on either side. The lift wasn't always working. We were there during the 1971 power cuts and often had to climb the concrete stairs in pitch blackness, counting the flights and hoping we'd got the right floor. Penny once went into the wrong block altogether, breezed into someone else's flat and started unpacking her shopping to the occupier's consternation.

Walter Yeates, Chief Librarian at Blackburn, had with great foresight, advised us to get the most expensive house we could afford. We did the opposite; we went into the private rented sector. It was in its own way a mini romantic gesture, an echo of what Dad had done when he bought 930. We rented a country cottage.

Approach Blackburn from the west, along Preston New Road, and a keen eye will spot a line of grey near the leafy summit of Billinge Hill. These are the cottages known as Billinge Side, formerly Freezeland Row. The first three in the row were owned by a woman who lived on Wyfordby Avenue, who had them given as a wedding present. She rented them out.

They were small, only suitable for couples or single people, but their situation was attractive and the view stretched across the Lancashire Plain to where the setting sun glinted on the Irish Sea. There was a glass-roofed kitchen extension at the back, which became stifling in hot weather and then a short, steep garden to the wall that ran round Billinge Wood. I used to climb the wall and heave Bess, our bull terrier, over too when I was taking her for a walk in the evening.

Despite fairly close supervision by the owner and some hostility from neighbours I liked living there. I liked getting to know the area. This is the part of Blackburn long colonised by the wealthy. Here were the big houses: Troy, Billinge Scar, Beardwood, Woodfold Hall, homes of millionaire cotton magnates and brewers. Here dwelt the Coddingtons, the Rutherfords and the Hornbys There was a 'trespassers will be shot' air about the place still. I found my way down to the ruins of Billinge Scar and examined the mosaic floor there. It was the former home of brewer Daniel Thwaites, reputedly the third richest person in the country in his day, after Queen Victoria and the Duke of Westminster. I penetrated as far as the grounds of Woodfold, but all the while feared a mantrap was waiting, with open jaws, or gamekeepers were preparing an ambush.

We were there about three years and then Jonathan was born and, without transport, it was difficult getting up and down the lane, especially with a pram. There were no pavements and motorists fairly flew along. It was 1974 and property prices had just begun that inexorable rise that was to change the way everybody lived. Housing costs had been negligible; we'd paid £16 per month for our council flat, which included rates. The house at Billinge Side was £20 per month. I was earning about £1,700 a year; housing costs were about one eighth of my income. Today I pay £600 a month rent; half my income.

Penny gave up work to look after Jonathan. House prices were already getting scary in Blackburn. Darwen was cheaper and the stone built terraces on the western side of the town more attractive than similar priced houses in Blackburn. We moved to Darwen

Men at Arms

For the Bronte children it was the gift of a box of toy soldiers that ignited their imaginations and led to a glorious blaze of melodramatic and romantic invention. The adventures they inscribed in their tiny notebooks were later distilled into the novels of their maturity. I'd like to be able to say that it was the gift of a box of soldiers that launched my own career of the imagination, but it would not be true. For me it was different.

Toy soldiers were made of lead and were painted all ready for the parade ground when I was a boy. They scorned khaki and camouflage and defied the enemy in scarlet uniforms and black busbies. Some wore kilts. Some held swords. Some carried rifles. Some carried musical instruments. I wasn't too keen on these. I could imagine the others in hand to hand combat, but not those with brass instruments to their lips.

They were soldiers of the Empire, symbols of the era when

Britain ruled, and Britain's values - the public school ones of decency, honour and courage were admired and envied by the whole world. Even the principal manufacturer of toy soldiers was called Britains

The biggest and best display of toy soldiers ever was mounted every Christmas at Busby's department store in Manningham Lane in Bradford.

I remember Bradford when everything was black. The Town Hall was black and so were all the warehouses around it. On a corner opposite the Town Hall was a Dickensian antique shop, full of ancient weapons, battered pewter, musty books, curious alabaster figures and dingy furniture. There were underground toilets nearby. Trolley buses wheezed stealthily to and fro.

Shopping in Bradford was always a torment. This was in the pre-supermarket days, when you got meat at the meat market, fish at the fish market and bread and pies at the bakers. The steep hills of Ivegate and Sunbridge Road, so taxing for youthful legs, led usually only to the horrors of an afternoon going round Rawson's meat market while Dad inspected the stalls for a suitable joint of beef for Sunday dinner.

But at Christmas time I didn't mind the steep climbs, because they led to Manningham Lane and Busby's. The store had a long frontage, half a dozen or more huge display windows and at the front of every one was a parade of toy soldiers in their scarlet and black, marching along with a stiff-backed precision that would have brought tears to the eye of a parade ground sergeant-major. Their deployment in a non toy store setting made them seem even more wonderful. What did they do with them the rest of the year? Would they lend them to me? I'd take good care of them.

And yet glorious as such a spectacle was and much as I admired my own miniature army, even more exciting things were in the offing. In 1953 the toy company Timpo, based in Scotland, brought out a series of knights of the Round Table. Made of lead of course, they came wrapped in tissue paper in their own individual boxes. Each was painted in its own heraldic colours. Sir Percival was in blue and white. Sir Lancelot was in red and gold. Sir Mordred and Sir Gawaine were available too. The horses and knights were all cast in the same attitudes, only the colours were different, and yet that was enough to give them their distinct characteristics, as they cantered over the lino to meet in mortal combat, or went seeking dragons to slay under the sideboard. The early models had metal lances, the later ones were plastic. And the coming of plastic was to change everything.

Lead soldiers were vulnerable, their heads were always the first to go. Unlike with real soldiers though, this was not a terminal injury. Heads could be secured again by means of a bit of matchstick. Bayonets soon got bent, and when you got tired of carefully replacing your soldiers in their display box, and chucked them in the toybox with their fellows, the paintwork soon suffered. Smart guardsmen became battle-scarred, leaden-hued old sweats, their heads lolling drunkenly and their bayonets drooping. Plastic promised a new era.

Plastic soldiers were cheaper; their colours were more vivid; their detail was finer; their aggressive postures more convincing. There were still guardsmen in their scarlet and black, but now there were Desert Rats, GI's, Germans and Japs. Carpet warfare now mirrored the real thing. It was no longer a matter of the troops of Empire marching round and round the settee terrifying the natives. Now there were machine gunners in the cushions and troops with bazookas and flame throwers in the deep pile of the hearth rug. Past conflicts were possible in plastic too - Confederates and Unionists, Prussians, Wellington's Guardsmen and the Imperial Guard of Napoleon. Timpo brought out a series of plastic knights in vivid colours, and, later, 'Swoppets' with movable and detachable accoutrements.

Plastic might have been a more appropriate medium, a happy medium, to express the cheapness of a soldier's life, but it lacked the gravitas, the monumental quality of lead. Timpo's new knights were moulded in more energetic postures, later models were even posable, but the very immobility and weight of the old knights seemed to give them authenticity - that was how knights were: heavy, awkward, clumsy.

It was an evening like any other. I was at Horton Bank Top Primary School then, no homework in those days, but nothing much on TV. After Childrens' Hour there was news, current affairs, documentaries, programmes devised and made with stuffy seriousness, not accessible to children as many programmes are today. Reading had yet to grab me. It was dull. I can still remember the dullness. It must have weighed heavily on my infant soul - all those dull weekday evenings and dull Sundays. Sunday evening was the dullest time of all.

Someone knocked at the door - a workmate of Dad's, nothing to interest me. I could hear them exchanging banter on the doorstep. Dad invited him in, but he couldn't stop. When Dad came back into the living room, he was carrying a big box.

"Here you are. It's Christmas come early. Fred's brought these round. They were their Malcolm's, but he never plays with'em now, so they want'em out of t'road."

It was a big, grey box, the kind of box a fur might arrive in, though Fred's wife Lucy didn't have one. My Auntie Elsie did and was envied and called behind her back for it. When she died, it went to my Mum, who didn't like it and made it into a rug. Later, as a would-be hippy, I made a waistcoat out of it.

It was a weight whatever it was. Dad put it down on the rug and I got my fingers under the lid and eased it off.

If it had been a casket of treasure my astonishment would have been illumined in a glow of gold and gems. Illumined or not it was treasure to me - the box was packed with soldiers. There were lead soldiers and plastic soldiers, knights, cowboys, red Indians, the 8th Army, the 7th Cavalry, the XXXth Legion, Arabs on camels, Cossacks on horseback, lancers, bombardiers and pikemen, snipers and swordsmen, artillery men and stretcher-bearers. There were horses without riders and riders without horses. There were soldiers who had lost their weapons, soldiers who had lost their limbs, soldiers who had lost their heads. Some had had their paintwork rubbed off. Some had never been painted. The bottom of the box was littered with body-parts.

It took me all night to assemble an inspection parade of my new army, and several days for the wonder to fade. Well, in a way it never has faded, and here I have to own up. Momentous as it was the moment did not contain that otherworldly ingredient. It was not an epiphany, not really a magic moment, by my definition, it was a moment of unlooked for joy nevertheless.

Little Book Man

Victoria Hall in Queensbury was my first library. There were only a few shelves of childrens' books. I have a recollection of crouching to examine them, with tall bays of grown-ups' books towering above me in the shadows.

When we moved, Great Horton Library in Bradford became part of my life. Inherited deference ensured that I felt I had no real right to be there. I didn't know how to search for books. Although the catalogue was out in the middle of the floor, I didn't know it was for public use and wouldn't have known how to use it if I had done. I didn't know you could ask the staff for help, or ask for books to be reserved

There was a Boots subscription library in Bradford. I looked round it from time to time, but never used it. Bradford's Central Library used to be in the same building as the Kirkgate Market. It seemed to be wrapped around the market somehow. I have only dim recollections of visiting it. The new Bradford Library, a big concrete and glass cliff-face, opened in 1966. It was a bold stride into the future. It was as exciting as a major airport. There were panoramic views of the city. Students were at work on every floor. There was a café. There was a theatre. The in and out counters were like supermarket checkouts. There were books. Of course there were books, but they were not easy to find, not for diffident, recreational readers anyway. There was a general library on the ground floor, but the rest of the building seemed to be for more serious users: students and researchers.

A chief librarian is something to be, as John Lennon might have put it. Maybe it's not the most glamorous, high-profile career, but when all the world's knowledge and all the world's stories are in books, having charge of them is not a role to be despised. That was true in ancient times, true right up to the nineteenth century and most of the way through the twentieth but, by the time I entered the profession, things were beginning to change. Bookmen were being replaced by managers; running a library was becoming much like running a supermarket: make sure the staff are doing their job and don't run out of baked beans, or, in a library, Mills and Boon romances.

My first job was at Blackburn and these changes were still some years away. Walter Yeates, the Chief Librarian, was a book man with a vision, with a mission: to promote his library, to do it his way. And it was his library and he did do everything his way. Most of the staff were scared of him. Everybody knew he couldn't be ignored; his bustling, bad-temper was omnipresent. He had that knack of being there when things were going wrong. He once threatened his Deputy, the Reference Librarian and myself with dismissal because at the Annual Book Exhibition he'd come across a display case of rare books unattended. He would ring the library at eight o clock at night to make sure staff had not gone home early, or he would appear in person, straightening calendars, picking up toffee papers, shouting at staff who might be engaged in personal conversations. In 1974 Blackburn Library Service was taken over by Lancashire County.

When I started in 1971 the library was in Library Street in the building opened in 1874. Borrowers did not have access to the books then. They queued at a counter and asked an assistant to retrieve them. Consequently the library was built as a warehouse, with shelves right up to the ceiling. When 'open access' came in 1925, the library had to be somehow reorganised so that the public could use it. Tall shelving, apart from in the stacks, was no longer suitable. Almost overnight the building became inadequate.

The reference department, run since just after the First World War by Dick Parkinson, colonised the whole building and the admin building opposite. There were dozens of sequences and getting to know them required a long apprenticeship. Most didn't like working in ref, but those of us who persevered felt like an elite, like Battle of Britain pilots, or young hospital interns. We would lounge negligently in the staff room, making casual references to esoterica: 'Rubber and Plastic Research Association Abstracts,' 'Skinner's Register' and 'Chetham's Miscellanies'.

It was a serious business working in a major library with regional responsibilities, only Manchester was larger. Blackburn took national papers and regional ones too - 'The Western Mail,' 'The Scotsman,' 'The Glasgow Herald.' It had bound back-files of learned journals, abstracts and indexes. It had telephone books for major foreign capitals. It had Extel cards and British Standards. It subscribed to HMSO publications. All this was underpinned by the collections bequeathed by Blackburn philanthropists: the Hart bequest, the Thompson bequest, the Dunne collection - private libraries built up over many years by enthusiastic bibliophiles. These were supplemented by the acquisition policies of a succession of keen bookmen, from WA Abram, David Geddes, Richard Ashton, James Hindle, John Walter Thomas to WW Yeates and his successor JB Darbyshire. From 1860 to 1974 when local government reorganisation changed everything these seven created and maintained the library - the 'magnificent seven.'

The Reference Library had the collected works of major writers,

Dickens, Eliot, Scott etc, but minor ones too - Bulwer Lytton, Harrison Ainsworth, Edwin Waugh. It had collected works of French, German, Spanish and Italian writers. There were county and town histories for most of Britain. There were works on botany, biology, ornithology, geology, geography, chemistry, physics. There were the published series of learned societies, complete runs of 'Whitaker's Almanac,' 'The Annual Register,' 'The Illustrated London News' and 'Punch'. There were books published by private presses, first editions, art books and rare books of engravings.

When you went into the stack, you were aware of all this accumulated knowledge, touched by it. It was an exhilarating experience. There was a buzz, an electric sensation - the wisdom leeched from the tightly packed pages in needles of fire and light.

Expansion had been talked about for years, but in the 1970s the search was on for new premises. WW Yeates wanted to be in the new shopping centre that was being built on the site of the old market and Thwaites Arcade. The Co-op got the site he had his eye on, and the library got the old Co-op Emporium in Town Hall St. For WW, along with the local government changes, it must have seemed as though all he had been struggling for was coming to an end, coming to nothing. Unable to contemplate serving under a County Librarian, and feeling himself too old to take on that role himself, he retired. He put it all behind him, devoted himself to fishing and was never seen in the library again.

The library moved in the summer of 1975 and it seems to me now as though that were the summer of my life, a summer that marked the end of an era, like those golden summers before the First World War, when human innocence was lost for ever.

I've never been wholeheartedly an office worker, a white-collar worker. The urge to be doing, digging, making, mending has always been there. Moving the library then was my chance. Great musty tomes had to be mined from the cellars of the building. Bound volumes of newspapers had to be brought out and passed from hand to hand in a human chain. Whenever I could, I got to the head of the chain, at the book-face, and passed back two, and sometimes three, of the heavy volumes, and enjoyed the groans and cries of protest from the weaker links, the ones unfamiliar with manual work.

There was a lorry on loan from the Building Department, but sometimes it was quicker just to run with a full trolley down King William Street, up Town Hall Street and in through the new glass doors, into that building where joiners and carpet fitters were still at work, where there was that smell: wood, glue, new carpet getting hot in the sun. On the second floor, where the Reference Library was, the ranks of grey, steel shelves had been erected, but they all had to be readjusted to accommodate oversized items. Was there going to be enough room?

There was unlimited overtime and I was happy doing over 70 hours a week. The old library was beginning to look bare. There were echoes. It looked smaller without the books, not bigger. Oddly the new library too was beginning to look smaller, as it filled up. The sun still shone. It was good to sit on the back of the lorry, keeping the trolleys under control, as it swung round the corner, and then to operate the tail-gate like a real worker.

A problem had cropped up in the Reference Library: engineers had decided the floor wouldn't bear the weight, so steel plates had to put in place under the feet of the laden shelves. Trolleys of books kept arriving, and still more. Was there going to be enough room?

A computerised issue system was installed. It had nothing to do with us. Reference staff were skilled in the ways of books: we didn't need computers. We were not Luddites however; microfilming was the coming thing and we had new readers to install and get used to. Furniture had to be deployed; desks and counters set up. Teams of staff began fine-tuning the arrangements of books. And still it was hot, and still the books kept coming. Was there going to be enough room?

There was enough room - just. When the last books had been placed on the last shelf, the Reference Library was full, no room for expansion. How were we going to cope? What was the place going to look like in a few years, if it continued to grow as it had been doing? The old building had managed to absorb 100 year's of growth; would this one? In the event it didn't matter.

The new building was very popular. There were queues. The shelves in the lending library were stripped bare, and extra supplies had to be shipped in from Preston. Students queued up for seats and study carrels. Many had to work sitting on the floor. There were constant tours and visits by groups. Harold Wilson, accompanied by fiery Barbara Castle officially opened the library on the 17th of October 1975. He had a further engagement in Bradford, so wasn't there long. When he left the staff were let loose on the food and wine with results that no less a writer than Lorenzo Dali has chronicled.

Something was left behind in the old library, something original, something essential, something that could never be recovered. Libraries were changing. Things would never be the same again.

Driving Ambitions

It would have been a pram; my first means of transport; a perambulator, a sort of distant cousin to the zinc bath in the cellar, only much grander, with gleaming coachwork and carriage wheels. There would have been a hood with a row of rattles, spanning my view of the sky, except when it was wet and then a waterproof cover would have eclipsed all.

I always wanted a pedal-car, one like Noddy's, being envious of the freedom it gave him, even if it landed him in the dark, dark wood, or the equally sinister, village of bouncing balls, but at Christmas I got clockwork trains, or Meccano: Dad had no use for a pedal car.

When we lived in Bradford I got a tricycle and a scooter. On May Day at school we used to trim our vehicles up with ribbons and have a procession around the nearby streets. It took me forever to learn to ride a bike, but when I did I got a sturdy two-wheeler with straight handlebars and Sturmey Archer gears. Later I got a BSA tourer with drop handlebars and five speed Deraillieur gears. It was on this bike that I got my first glimpse, first sensation of freedom, freedom from the limitations of my body, freedom to fly.

I would go out early in the morning, drawn back to Queensbury. On one such occasion it was sunny and warm and I paused on Roper Lane, with its view over Halifax, and it hit me that my bounds had become unbounded, that all horizons were attainable, my wheels could circle the globe - provided there wasn't too much traffic. Even though it was a climb up Great Horton Bank, I preferred it to going downhill towards the maelstrom of traffic that seethed around the city centre.

Sutcliffe had a car. My friend Christopher Kellett's Dad, Bert, had a car - a timber clad shooting brake. He owned a stationery business in Bradford. Sometimes I'd be invited out with them for a country run at the weekend. I used to be scared of him, but I was easily scared.

Dad didn't get a car until I was well into my teens - a maroon Austin Cambridge, as solid as a tank. He got Sutcliffe to give him a few lessons, not that Sutcliffe had ever passed a test, but if you'd had a licence since the 1930s, you didn't need to. It was strange to see Dad not in control, not coping very well.

We used to play chess and at first he always beat me, but once I beat him and realised I could do so fairly easily, I didn't play him again. I couldn't bear to see him as anything less than omnipotent, though I don't think he was bothered. And when I had children of my own I realised that you're quite pleased that they can do things better than you can.

Dad passed his test at the second attempt and soon after swapped The Austin Cambridge for a big, blue Ford Zodiac with wings. He was signalling something here, as he had done when he bought 930 Great Horton Road. He wanted life on a larger scale. He wanted another dimension. He wanted to fly.

I was a student at Leeds Polytechnic by then and, unlike now when college car parks are full, nobody had a car, nor a motor bike, nor a scooter. Graham Midgeley did, who'd been with me at Cooper Lane School, Horton Bank Top, Grange Grammar School and now Leeds, but he was doing a business degree and they were a different kind of student.

I was still car-less after college. Car ownership was not so widespread in the 1970s. You could still see streets without a car parked in them. I have a photograph of Cyprus Street in Darwen with not a car in sight. How different it looks, how handsome. This was how it was meant to look.

We had a car briefly when we lived on Billinge Hill. Sadly though it only left the garage once, and then not all of it did.

Penny's family had long felt we should have a car, especially after Jonathan was born and in the end her father Norman gave us his old one when he changed it - a dark green Hillman Minx.

A garage came with the cottage. It was at the other side of the road, at the top of a grassy slope that swept down to Meins Road. Penny went off for her first lesson. The car had a starting handle. It occurred to me that the battery might go flat, so I checked to see if there was enough room at the front for the starting handle to go in, there wasn't, but if the car could be backed up a couple of inches...

I'd sat in the Austin Cambridge and Dad had gone through the basics, so theoretically I knew what I was doing. I started her up. Two problems : I knew nothing about clutch control and I'd left the driver's door open. The clutch flew up, the car lurched backwards, the door pierced the asbestos wall of the garage, went right through and doubled back on itself, crumpling the wing. The grassy knoll rushed up. Mercifully I managed to push the clutch back in and brake.

I was in a panic. My leg was dithering. I put the car in first gear and tried to inch slowly forward back into the garage. Again the clutch flew up. The car slammed into the garage wall, cracking it. The door came back through the side wall squealing in protest. I switched off the engine and crawled out. The door wouldn't shut.

When Penny came back full of enthusiasm after her driving lesson, I had to tell her I'd written off the car without getting it out of the garage, written off the garage too. No more was said about cars and learning to drive.

Years went by and one day, in dawn's sickly hue, when I'd come round from my Strongbow stupor, I lay awake and pondered my transportless existence. Everybody I knew had cars. Nobody lived within walking distance: Ringo was at Tosside, Tony and Linda at Tottington, Dave and Gerry in Blackburn; my family in Bradford. I was always being picked up and dropped off, like someone elderly and infirm. It was unfair on them and bad for my self-respect. Learning to drive a car, passing the test seemed a lot of bother, a nerve-wracking business that could take months. Besides I didn't see myself as a car owner. What did I need a car for, I was on my own? I wanted something that would express my individuality. I decided to get a motorbike.

In those days a learner could ride a bike up to 250 cc. I knew Vin Cunningham who had the motorbike shop in Blackburn Road in Darwen. He was a friend of Mary Grogan's at Darwen Library. His earnest clergyman's look belied a sharp sense of humour. I bought a black Suzuki 200SB from him. What a beast it seemed, a great, roaring monster that could blast everything off the road. Vin delivered bikes for beginners to the training session at Shadsworth School that took place on a Saturday morning. Volunteers put you through the basics and got you weaving between cones.

I was the oldest there by a long way. I wasn't a natural. I was too nervous, too hesitant, my balance wasn't good. Anyway I was let go at last and wobbled and wove my way back to Darwen. It was the right turn from busy Blackburn Road into Sunnyhurst Lane that I dreaded and rightly so. I was waiting in the middle of the road, when a car stopped and flashed his lights for me to go. I lurched forward, stalled and fell over. An amused passer-by helped me to my feet and got my bike upright for me. I felt like the White Knight in 'Alice Through the Looking Glass.'

That bike terrified me, but every day I made myself go out on it. Everyday with misgivings, I would don my helmet, motorbike boots and gauntlets, and clunk down the iron steps at the side of my flat, kick-start the bike into a roar and wobble out into the road. I persevered until I was just about fit to be on the road. I passed my test at the second attempt. The first time I misunderstood the examiner's instructions and lost him - not good to return to the test centre separately.

Later I got a 250 cc X7 and later still Suzuki GS425E. I never got on a bike without a frisson. I'd no confidence. I could see danger round every bend, maybe that's what saved me from an accident, though I came off a few times, once when I left the side stand down - you tend not to do that more than once.

I went up to Scotland, down to Warwickshire and frequently over to Yorkshire, not only to see family, but to see Keith and Rita who lived in North Anston at the other side of Sheffield. Keith had been at Leeds Poly with me. Both he and his wife were ex-bikers and took a keen interest in my bike. Keith insisted on trying it out and was gone for ages. I feared the worst. He had dropped it, but apart from a bent lever and a bent pedal, no great harm was done.

I was leaving there one winter morning. Rita made me a flask of hot coffee. The cold's always a problem on a bike; even on a fine day sticking to the speed limit you're riding into the teeth of a 30 mph wind. This morning wasn't fine. It was cold, wet and miserable. It was wet still in Sheffield and going up the M1, but in the Pennine hills it was snowing. I stopped at Delph above Oldham to have a warming drink. Unfortunately I had full-face helmet on and my fingers were too numb to undo the straps. I carried on. I'm sure it's possible to die of hypothermia on a bike.

I still had a bike when I met my second wife, Fiona. Riding with a pillion passenger requires all kinds of adjustments as regards balance, stopping and starting. My first experience had been on the SB200 when I took Ringo up to Tosside.

It was a cold winter's day again and we were both muffled up. I didn't have a proper spare helmet, only an old-fashioned peaked thing, the sort that George Formby might have worn. It was too small and sat on his head like a pea on a drum. We made sedate, but safe progress as far as the big roundabout on the A59 just north of Langho. Through some lack of co-ordination, or communication we glided to a halt, but neither of us put a foot down. We capsized as though we'd been holed below the water-line.

Babies and bikes don't mix. When Fiona got pregnant, it was time to rethink. Through some legal loophole you could drive a three-wheeler then with a motorbike licence. I sold the bike to Dave Wilson and bought one.

It was that that gave me my first taste of the exhilaration of motoring. I was driving up the A59 with Pendle in view. It was a sunny day. Such was my sense of freedom, such was my joy at it all, that I stopped in a lay-by to savour it, savour the moment.

There I was with my hands resting on the wheel of my pea-green Reliant Robin saloon - the world was at my feet. Thus was my appetite for the open road born.

Christmas in Hospital

How Lucozade has changed! Once it was an elixir, a specific remedy at times of sickness, obtainable only from chemists. The bedside ritual of opening the bottle had all the gravity of a medical procedure. Mum would unwrap the cellophane, unwind the foil cap, remove the black stone stopper and pour the effervescing liquid into the glass, where it would seethe and rage. A fizzing half tumbler would be administered, never a full glass. After a blissful sip I'd place the glass on my bedside table to subside a little while I straightened out the foil into a circle, and then held up the cellophane to my eyes to get a jaundiced view of my sickroom. Now Lucozade's in a plastic bottle on the shelves of every supermarket and promoted as a sport's drink, an everyday sort of drink.

Oh the deliriums of childhood sickbeds. Oh the fevered imaginings. The patterns of the wallpaper and the curtains would unravel and knit themselves into malevolent expressions - ghouls, goblins, and at night they would drop to the floor and congregate at my bedside chanting and gibbering. And oh the thirst! Is there anything sweeter than slaking a feverish thirst?

Drinking's one of the first things we do. We don't even have to learn. We know how to do it, just as we know how to breathe and our heart knows how to beat. It is life itself. We soak it up as dry land soaks up the rain. No judicious ruminating, you just throw back your head and let it flow into you, a total surrendering to experience

Pop was a great childhood pleasure. We used to get it delivered by Stanton's. It came in stone jars, later glass. We got Ben Shaws pop too from the shop on the corner of Bartle Lane and Gt Horton Road. It came in quart bottles with a stone stopper. There was grapefruitade, and orangeade and dandelion and burdock and sarsaparilla and ginger beer and shandy gaff and lemonade, both white and yellow.

Sutcliffes used to get Boococks pop from Boothtown. They had more flavours - pineapple, lime, and it came in pint bottles. There were mixed fruit drinks like Vimto and Tizer, but I've no recollection of Coca Cola as a child. Now Coke is ubiquitous and many regional pop manufacturers have gone.

In adult life we come to terms with traumas, develop strategies for dealing with 'outrageous fortune.' There's not much to protect you when you're a child; like a moon with no atmosphere to burn up incoming meteors, everything leaves its mark, even the meanest meteorites.

One of the severest traumas of my childhood came at the age of eight, when I was sentenced to an indefinite stay at Woodlands Orthopaedic Hospital at Rawdon. I remember going round Bradford before catching the bus up there, with permission to buy something to console myself. I ended up clutching a pair of Cisco Kid revolvers and a Donald Duck cartoon book, which had a creepy story about Donald going to a castle haunted by skeletons.

I was there for four months and I suppose sort of got used to it, but I never felt accepted by my fellows on the ward, some who had been there for years. One in particular I remember. I picture him as a homunculus, red-faced and wry-limbed, a malevolent Uriah, who could not keep the stopper on his spite. He preferred to use it as a weapon. It was a stone stopper from a pop bottle and he launched it with devilish accuracy. It flew and struck home with the force of years of accumulated bile.

I was pouring a glass of Lucozade. The stone missile struck and shattered the bottle, blasting me with orange fizz spiked with shards of glass. The ward acclaimed his skill with a roar. 'Well struck sir!' was the gist of it.

What with outpatients appointments and physiotherapy, hospitals came to seem part of my life, but it wasn't until 1971 when I moved to Blackburn that I was an in-patient again.

I missed the Blackburn of the Thwaites Arcade and the Market Hall Tower by a few years. By the time I arrived the new shopping centre was in place, the tiled warren, the like of which was soon to be found in every town in the land. The great wall of Debenhams was there too, a wall which divided the town centre in half, separating King William Street from Church Street..

I didn't miss the old library though which was still in its Library Street premises, shared with the museum. What a warren that was, though an enchanting, book-lined one that went up and down mezzanines, climbed into attics and dived into cellars.

The library was cultivating a remarkable crop of young men: Andy Holliday, Stephen Child, Pete Hinchley, Jim Heyes, Bob Snape, all of whom would go on to distinguished careers in the profession. They worked hard and they played hard, and I got swept along in their slipstream. At lunchtime we would go to the Ying Kin Chinese restaurant above the new market hall and have the special three course lunch and a couple of pints. How did I manage that? Now half a cheese sandwich and I'm uncomfortably full.

They all had Minis and in the evening we'd pack into Andy's or

Stephen's or Pete's and whizz out of town to the Bonnie Inn at Salesbury, or the Royal Oak at Riley Green, or the other Royal Oak at Longsight Road. On one such evening, not long before Christmas we were in the Bonnie Inn. It was packed. I didn't feel well. Slade's latest Christmas hit had the crowd swaying gently like underwater creatures in a current. I just thought how mad it was for us all to be packed in here when there were cold dark fields outside, where a man could cool down and be at peace. I wasn't well.

The next day at the Doctor's I was diagnosed with acute appendicitis and an ambulance was called to the surgery. They operated later the same day. So Christmas in hospital loomed. Everybody said it would be good; a surgeon would come on to the ward and facetiously carve the turkey. There would be plenty of booze, and the nurses would be adorned with tinsel and mistletoe. I wasn't convinced. The eight year old boy confined to Woodlands was coming out in me.

And when *the* moment came, it was shot through with poignancy rather than joy. It was in the evening. Visiting was over. I was on ward five gazing, half-dozing, at the canal and the lights of Mill Hill, with the bulk of Billinge Hill, a black shape against the starry sky.

I heard the first note when they were some distance away, and yet thought it came from further away still - something of angel voices was in it. The singing came nearer. The hair crawled on my scalp. Nurses were walking the wards, singing and bearing candles.

"It came upon the Midnight clear, while glory shone around."

The glory of candle flame shone around them, making of them wraiths as they walked by my bed. These were nurses I'd seen skylarking in the sluices, now transformed in their cloaks and solemnity, their eyes lambent in the candle flames, like new brides of Christ.

"Silent night, Holy night.
All is calm, all is bright"

I had to look away. It was all but unbearable. For a moment the spirit of Christmas filled the ward, filled me too with a sweet sadness.

They moved on and their voices faded, echoing as though they had returned to heaven. I stared out into the night and the orange lights of Blackburn were starred with tears.

Breakfast at Cayton Bay

It was always better when there was someone else there. Maybe there was a time when I didn't think that, when it was enough for there to be just Mum and Dad and me, but as far back as I can remember I preferred there to be company. The atmosphere was a bit thin when there was just the three of us, four after Linda was born. There was a sense of oppressiveness, a suffocating sense of a looming vacuum, as though we'd drifted too far from the warmth of convivial company and good fellowship, and were approaching a void.

I'm tempted to say Dad liked company and Mum didn't, but it wasn't quite so simple. Maybe she didn't like his kind of company - his family and his workmates. She had her own friends: Annie Woolley, Miss Liversedge, but she was certainly negative when get-togethers were in the offing and there'd be a row; she sulking; Dad shouting. That was another good reason for liking company:

it stopped them rowing. I always loved people coming, always hated it when they left. What could be better than company being on holiday with us?

Women can somehow influence seemingly dominant husbands and lead them in the way they want them to go. Mum was never fond of boarding houses. Staying at them required sociability, especially in the morning at breakfast time, when she preferred to be silent and glum. It meant being at the mercy of the culinary skills of the landlady. Mum never liked runny fried eggs and at one establishment asked if hers could be turned over. The landlady gave her a funny look but agreed and the next morning Mum's runny egg was upside down on the plate.

We started to go self-catering, which in the 1950s meant caravans or chalets. There was a big caravan park at Cayton Bay, a bus-ride south of Scarborough, though it was walkable and we often did walk. That became our holiday destination for many years and one year we invited the Sutcliffes.

Certain things were only done 'en famille' in those days. Having meals was one of them. People would come to tea, but that was a special ritualised event, not like having people share a family meal. Everybody knew what to expect when they came to tea - boiled ham, or tongue, or luncheon meat, or corned beef, and salad - a tomato and a piece of lettuce. There would be bread and butter, and cake - madeira, or sponge, or battenberg. There would be tea in the best cups and saucers.

Daringly my parents broke with tradition and made a proper roast beef dinner once when the Sutcliffes came. You should have seen their faces. Sutcliffe set too with gusto. He loved anything novel. Audrey was less keen. She probably thought she'd be expected to reciprocate. One thing about the traditional tea - it required no planning, no skill. You gave nothing away. You didn't reveal your shortcomings. Needless to say we didn't have Yorkshire pudding with our roast beef dinner.

Sutcliffe's response was innovative too. He took us to a Chinese restaurant in Halifax - the 'Far East.' Eating out was not much done in our circle in those days, apart from the market pie and pea stalls, and fish and chip shops where you could eat in. Going out for a meal in the evening was not something we did. There was nowhere to go to for one thing. Berni Inns with prawn cocktail starters and chicken in a basket didn't get going until the 1960s. But by the late 50s Chinese restaurants had started to appear in towns and cities throughout the North. The English were starting to get adventurous about eating, some of them anyway. Sutcliffe of course tucked into Chicken Chow Mein with lychees to follow; Dad had steak and chips with ice cream. Mum had a plain omelet.

Going on holiday was also done 'en famille' in the 1950s, so more new ground was being broken. Holidays were exciting enough anyway, but having friends coming to stay made it doubly so.

Cayton Bay welcomed the sea with open arms. It had a wide, white empty beach, so different to Scarborough's, which was packed on fine days, and even on foul ones had its platoons of folk huddled behind windbreaks, or promenading, leaning into a wind that made their pacamacs rattle. The beach at Cayton Bay was always empty and even when it wasn't, it was so big it seemed so. There was a concrete pill-box at the south end to fire my imagination and from where I repulsed the invading Germans time and time again

On the campsite there were amusements, and stalls where you could buy seaside essentials - buckets and spades; flags; beach balls; fishing nets; cricket bats; sun-glasses; silly hats; postcards; souvenirs; car stickers and pennants and badges. There were stalls where you could get candyfloss; toffee apples; and rock novelties, and places where you could get cups of tea and fish and chips.

You could hire bikes and Dad did persevere with me, but I was hopeless. It took me longer to learn to ride a bike than it did to drive a car. We were still coming to Cayton Bay in 1964 when my sister Linda was nine. The Beatles were in the charts with 'Hard Day's Night.' It was being played all over the camp. That opening chord triggered all sorts of adolescent fantasies, triggered my own adolescence in many ways. Linda learned to ride a bike that holiday. It took her half a day.

Sutcliffe had a car. He had had a motorbike for a while and when they came to visit, he would come on the bike and Audrey and the girls would come on the bus. His car was a 1940s Morris Ten saloon with blue bodywork and black mudguards.

I waited at the entrance to the caravan site, thinking every car that approached was theirs. It was like watching for a kettle to boil. But then there they were at last. Sutcliffe sounded his horn with a flourish, arms were waving from every window. He'd fitted racy white-wall tyres - on three of the wheels anyway.

It was a small caravan, and when our guests were inside with their cups of tea and all their luggage, it was clear just how small it was. It was going to require some ingenuity to make sleeping arrangements. I slept on the floor with my legs down the stair-well, but that was all part of the fun.

Next day dawned warm and sunny, and we could spill out on to the grass and ease the pressure inside. There were one or two early birds making for the beach, one or two walking back from the shop with a paper. The smell of frying bacon was in the air. The whole day stretched ahead. No need to worry about family rows, or being bored. We'd all pile into Sutcliffe's car and be off.

Seven of us used to squeeze into that car. I used to sit in the front between Dad's legs, my nose inches from the windscreen. There were no seat-belts in those days, and with indifferent brakes and Sutcliffe's cavalier driving, it's a wonder I survived. On steep hills Sutcliffe would switch off the engine and coast to save petrol.

We'd be off, looking for new beaches, secret coves and caves. Maybe we'd find a beer-garden. Maybe we'd go down to Filey, or up to Whitby. When we got back after tea, there'd be time to go down to the beach. There was all the time in the world. It was a sunny summer day in childhood and it was going to go on for ever.

Sutcliffe appeared at the caravan door.

"Are you full of beans?" he asked.

I nodded.

"No you're not.   You haven't had any yet," he grinned and showed me the pan, where they were bubbling away.

And that was it.   That was the moment.   All this and beans for breakfast too.   I closed my eyes and looked at the sun.

Tinkle Tinkle Little Star

Only the spirit remains, only a recollection of emotion, a recollection that can cause a frisson even now. It was a carol service or rehearsal and we were in a chapel, or church. The hymn we were singing was 'O Come Emmanuel.' It was afternoon and growing dark. Christmas was in prospect. I was at Grange School, a silly thirteen year old, messing about with his mates, but just for a moment my giggles were silenced and I was touched by a sense of wonder.

Christmas could even transform school, just as snow makes something magical of a dreary urban landscape. We would get orange juice instead of milk in the days just before we broke up, and the caps would have a holly design. At infant and junior school there would be a Christmas party, and we would bring cake, or jelly, or sandwiches. Names would have to be taped on any plates that were brought. There would be carols at morning assembly. The classroom would be decorated. There would be the nativity play.

I've no recollection of Christmas at Queensbury Church School, but at Cooper Lane I remember the nativity play. Thankfully I was not cast in any major role, nor in any role at all. I was in charge of pulling back and closing the curtains and to do this I had to sit on a vaulting horse, or some tall item of gym equipment. I was given a signal when I had to start hauling. All went well, until I hauled away with too much enthusiasm and my bony knees were exposed to the full view of the audience, quite eclipsing the twinkling star, that the wise men were following.

At Horton Bank Top School my thespian skills were called upon at last. I got the part of a shepherd in the school's annual big production: The Nativity Play. My dread of the ordeal blotted out Christmas. Whereas I would normally be looking forward to Christmas as soon as my November birthday was over, now I could not. Christmas was locked away behind this awful barrier. It was as far away from me as it would have been in the bad old days of Oliver Cromwell, who banned it altogether.

I had some lines to learn, not many, but too many. They slipped and writhed out of my memory's grasp like greased eels. I knew the whole world would be watching, watching for me to make a mistake, waiting for me to dry up completely.

It's a natural thing not to want to be the focus of so many eyes, but I think my case was compounded by an earlier trauma. We moved from Queensbury around the time of my birthday and I started at Cooper Lane School. There was a custom there of calling on stage at morning assembly anybody whose birthday it was and singing Happy Birthday at them. My first day was my birthday and terrified as I was already, I had to face this. It was too much. My bladder couldn't cope.

Let me assure you that peeing yourself on stage in front of the whole school is not a good way to start your school career.

Christmas was coming, but so was the play. I actually became ill with a streaming cold, and although Dad was not one to permit time off through sickness, I think I could have got off, if I'd looked suitably wobbly and woebegone. I couldn't do it though. The play was too important and my role too vital. It was a command performance with God himself in the Royal Box, sure to give fierce critical attention to this dramatic reconstruction of events in which he had such a personal interest.

For a costume I wore my dressing gown and a piece of cloth tied round my head with a bit of fancy cord. All the shepherds had speaking parts, 'Lo, We were watching our flocks by night,' or some such, which they chanted in the traditional manner: an unnatural monotone. Of course it's not just a question of knowing your own lines, you have to know the lines of whoever speaks before you.

My turn came. There was a pause. I was concentrating on my lines, reciting them in my head, then, aware of expectant faces all around, I struggled to find my voice. It was a voice smothered in a cold.

'Behode liddle Jesus lyid in a major.'

There was another pause while the next speaker, a king in a magnificent gold crown made of cardboard, with a charcoal moustache, stared at me, wondering what on earth I was talking about. There was a bit of hissed prompting from the wings, and we were off again.

I'd done it. I'd done it. I hadn't forgotten my words. My bladder had coped. The relief was wonderful. Christmas could come now.

Years later I went to see a nativity play and my kids were in it - William as a wise man and Emily as Mary. It was charming, but so small scale and cosy. All the parents were kindly disposed, and any lapses of memory were greeted with affectionate good humour. And yet I could see the terror on William's face. How different everything seems from the perspective of an eight year old.

No nativity play at secondary school. There were Christmas exams, which in their own way acted as a barrier to Christmas.

After exams we could bring games to school, while the teachers did their marking. I suppose it saved them doing it at home

It seemed always to snow in those days. There were always snowball fights, always slides in the school playground, and sledging. We wore balaclavas and woolly gloves and wellies. Snow used to get wedged in them benumbing your instep.

But the carol service and 'Oh Come Emmanuel,' stand out. There, in that darkened, holy place was a moment of transcendence, a glimpse of cold, blue, numinous otherness, the infinite, that lies just beyond our reach.

A Christmas Carol

Possession - possessing something, owning it in an attempt to steal something permanent from the fleeting moment An illusion of course, nothing's permanent, everything changes, and time is the catalyst for change. Even those remarkable families, who still own the land given to them for manslaughter on a noble scale by William the Conqueror a thousand years ago, have not cheated time - for each individual there has come the moment when hands could no longer grasp, no longer cling on.

Maybe it was an awareness of this evanescence, of the temporary nature of all things, that led Dad to demur when I said I wanted a book for Christmas, or maybe it was because he was being asked to fork out 21 bob for a book, when you could get them free at the library.

There were two books in the house when I was little, both books of fairy stories that had been Mum's. I ruined them by scribbling on them with crayons, and she said she wished she'd never given them to me. I was too young. It was before I realized books were magic, that books could change who you were, where you were, when you were. My first book was a Noddy book.

I identified with Noddy. I was Noddy. I too would have planted toffees and expected a toffee tree to grow, if I'd had the wit to think of it, and if there'd been anywhere among the flags and cobbles to plant anything. I too would have found the village of bouncing balls scary, nightmarish in fact, and as for being stripped and left in the dark, dark wood in the middle of the night by jeering golliwogs who drove off in your car . . . What a potent mix of fears Enid Byton dreamt up there!

I thought Big Ears spoiled things. He was sanctimonious and insufferable, she should have killed him off and then see Noddy go! Look out Lord of the Flies!

As I've said, we used the library in Victoria Hall in Queensbury. There was a hush, an atmosphere there that was a long way from the bustle outside in Sandbeds - the clangor of the tram; the rattle of carts; the clip-clop of hooves; the ribaldry of the chip-shop queues, and the queues of men waiting for the Stag's Head to open.

Dad read too, westerns mainly. Mum had read romances once, but once she realised where such nonsense led, she read religious books. 'The Letters of the Scattered Brotherhood' was a favourite.

When we moved to Bradford I went to Cooper Lane School. In the infant classes, there was always a story at the end of the day. We used to sit on the floor round the teacher. The memory of her selecting which book to read is one of the few that carries me back to how it was at the time, how it felt to be sitting cross-legged on the floor at her feet.

We used Great Horton Library then. What excitement the rest of the weekend held, if I got a couple of good books. The thrill of an ardent collector lighting on a long-coveted treasure could be no greater than mine at finding a new Billy Bunter or William book. To have it in my hands, a title I'd never seen before, was a tangible excitement, no matter how dog-eared and stained it was, indeed that only added to its authenticity, its value - Billy Bunter and the Holy Grail!

Don't ask me why I was so enthralled by the public school antics of 'the Fat Owl of the Remove.' What was the 'Remove' anyway? And why did I identify with William Brown? They had servants! Would I have been any more enthralled if there'd been books in those days about kids whose parents worked in the mill, who ate their dinner at noon and had pigeons and toilets in their back yards?

I could disappear into a book then, be absorbed by it for hours, days. Not now, now my concentration is feeble. I'm easily distracted. I get uncomfortable. I fall asleep. I haven't time for reading. I should be washing, washing up, cleaning, doing something in the garden, or even writing. There isn't time when you're nearly sixty, only the young can spare the time to read.

Dad put some books in my way - Tarzan, Professor Challenger, westerns, notably ones with a character called Sudden. We used to get paperbacks from Stringer's in Kirkgate Market. I graduated early to the adult library at Great Horton. I started going in there to get westerns for Dad. They were shelved in author order with the rest of fiction, but had w on the spine. Later I started picking out books for myself.

I read fiction and non-fiction with equal enthusiasm. One week my favourite book would be 'My Family and Other Animals,' by Gerald Durrell, the next it would be 'Craig of the Welsh Hills,' by Roy Saunders. Dad's input apart, I found my own way about. I don't remember any help from school. I only remember Janet and John books from junior school and at grammar school we were offered 'The Secret Agent,' 'The Trumpet Major,' and 'The Cloister and the Hearth,' all good books of course, but too soon, far too soon.

Still not many books at home, apart from the library books that came and went. For some reason we had a copy of 'The Morning Will Come,' by Naomi Jacobs. I never looked into it, but took faint consolation from the title, as though it were a sampler on the wall - an improving motto.

There were annuals - Rupert, Dandy, Beano. It was the custom for my annual to be left on my bed during the night on Christmas Eve, so when I awoke I'd find it and know 'He'd been.' I remember the smell of them and the squeaky stiffness and the delight of knowing there'd be more stuff downstairs.

Buying things seemed to enhance Christmas. I suppose it gave it some permanence. I started to get Giles Annuals. They'd been going since the war. They drew a wry, but cosy picture of England, with the weather often featured: rain, fog - snow at Christmas time. We bought them before Christmas, part of the preparations, along with the Christmas issue of Radio Times and festive editions of magazines like Yorkshire Life and Reveille,and the comics with snow on the masthead.

The time came at last when all pretence of Father Christmas was gone. For a while my parents maintained the fiction that the toys were delivered on Christmas Eve by the catalogue company, but I found them hidden in the wardrobe one year and that was that. I enjoyed keeping up the pretence for my sister Linda though, and there were one or two Christmas Eves when I took part in the setting out of her presents after she'd gone to bed.

I used to go into to Bradford before Christmas with my Dad to choose something. It was 1960. I was twelve. Dad's patience was limited. I knew I couldn't take for ever making up my mind. We looked in Carters and Baines' and the toy stall on the market. We looked in Woolworth's and then the book department in Boots.

I knew 'A Christmas Carol' from the Alastair Sim film. I'd read it too and been terrified by Marley's ghost, a little bored by the Ghosts of Christmas Past and Christmas Present, but terrified again by the Ghost of Christmas Yet to Come. Boots had an edition of the book illustrated by Ronald Searle. It was the perfect thing. The cover alone glowed like a Christmas tree. His cartoon images brought a convivial warmth and humour that Dickens would have admired. The drawing of the mouse fainting at the sight of

Marley's ghost was not only amusing, but hinted at new depths, new angles.

Dad was not convinced - 21 bob for a book! - and books free at the library! He didn't refuse however and the book was mine. As we went into the dark December streets of Bradford with the starlings shrilling and the queues for buses bending back upon themselves outside the town hall. I had it in my hand - a treasure, a piece of Christmas you could touch. It was like a religious icon. I read it reverently. It became part of the ritual of Christmas, read every year, and though it no longer summons up the magic it once did, my responses having grown dull, it has a place of honour on my shelf to this day.

Four Ashes

Few of these moments have been inspired by alcohol. You need a clear head, a keen sense of perception. Alcohol is a fine fellow when the glasses are brimming and the fire's roaring in the grate, but a poor thing in the cold light of day, when your mouth tastes like a doormat and the ague is in every joint. You might have had a dozen magic moments the night before, but you wouldn't remember one. This is one I did remember, albeit hazily.

Pubs were for grown men in the 1950s and 60s. Women and young people were just tolerated. The idea of putting alcohol in pop to tempt teenagers would not have been acceptable. You had to acquire the taste. Your first sip was no more pleasant than your first puff on a cigarette, but you just had to persevere. Maybe I had a head start. There was always drink in the house, well it was always being bought, even if it was consumed straight away. From an early age I was allowed a sip, then a glass to myself, and then a bottle. Heys Gold Cup was the preferred tipple for weaning infants. It was not strong. Strengths were not given on labels then. If they're meant to serve as a warning now, they have the opposite effect.

We used to go in Brackenhill Park, Christopher Kellett and I, with a couple of bottles from the off-licence. I can still remember that off-licence/grocery smell, chiefly soap powder, but with other subtle influences. It was a smell encountered again later when I went to Graham Midgeley's, whose father was a grocer. Graham was left in charge sometimes when his parents were out, and we'd help ourselves to the draft sherry, or a miniature something or other, if we had the money.

There was a wide choice of bottled beers - Websters Green Label, White Rose No 5, Ramsdens Stone Trough. There was Whitaker's Cock of the North, Tetleys, Hammonds and John Smiths. There was pale ale, brown ale and stout. There was always the fear too that we wouldn't get served. We were fifteen and didn't look remotely like eighteen, but we usually got served.

We'd sit on the benches at the back of the park and look at the orange lights of Bradford spread out below us. We became adept at opening bottles on the tops of fence posts. We'd shiver and chatter and grow giddy on cold beer that was not much stronger than shandy.

Getting served in pubs required more nerve. Hard to look nonchalant under the satirical gaze of seasoned topers. Should you stand at the bar, lounge casually against it; or scurry out of sight, clutching your pint, its smooth sides slippery with foam? There was a drinking culture at school. The elite, the more sophisticated, would go in the town centre pubs, where there was a real chance of police raids and prosecution. We started out in the country pubs on our moorland walks, where the chance of a raid was negligible. At Ogden we favoured The Causeway Foot, with its flag floors and cosy rooms, The Withins too, though you could set out thither across the moortop and arrive with a keen thirst, only to find it closed. The Blackstone Edge was another favourite, though that was so small half a dozen drinkers would fill it. In Haworth we favoured the Fleece.

Great Horton Road, the A647, was our route to dissipation. Once these inns would have been welcome sights to travellers and coachmen. As Bradford grew, they would serve the communities that developed along the road. We knew all the pubs from Grange Road to Queensbury. A pint in all of them would have been beyond our capacity, beyond our pockets too, even though bitter was about 8p a pint then. My paper round money, 12/6, or 62p, could finance a night out with some to spare. We usually did about five or six, having a pint in each one.

There were three of us: Dave Buckley, Gordon Sanders, fellow classmates from Grange School, and myself. It was the talk we enjoyed as much as the beer, the schoolboy humour, the excitement of new ideas, new books - well ideas and books that were new to us. We were intoxicated as well by the new things that were happening to us, to our minds and our bodies, new understandings, new capabilities. The alcohol gave us wings, made us soar, made us eloquent, made us witty.

It was a Thursday night and we started at the Royal Hotel, a Websters house. Oh the pubs then - what dens of adventure, where the shadows of intrigue still lingered, where whispers of conspiracy still echoed. Now they've been opened out - big, square, carpeted spaces filled with noise and light. There are no snugs, no selects, no nooks where old men can doze, no roaring taproom fires where coachmen can warm their cold backsides.

It was a dark December evening with snow threatening. Not many in the Royal and the landlord seemingly happy for it to stay like that. Nevertheless he relinquished his Telegraph and Argus and served us. Websters bitter had a sharp, sour, yeasty smack to it. The drinking was competitive - who could drink fastest; who could drink most; who could hold their drink best; who could avoid being sick at the end of the night. We were like young bucks play-fighting, learning, learning how to use alcohol as a transforming medium as it was used once by ancient people, whose shadowy presences is felt most of all as the sun dies and the winter solstice approaches. Maybe such shadowy presences were watchful that night and approving as we drank and acted the goat.

The George and Dragon next, which was aspiring to be the kind of pub we have today, open-plan, with a central bar, upholstered seats, brasses and prints on the walls. Even the beer was aspirational. It was the equivalent of alcopops. Beer was being made palatable to the young - light, fizzy, cold and bland. There was Watneys Red Barrel, Whitbread Tankard, Gauntlet, Worthington E. Not only were these beers designed to suit naïve palettes, but the brewers' accountants too; keg beer lasted longer than traditional ale, so there was less waste. The George and Dragon was for couples, young couple, middle aged couples, old couples. We moved on.

Did we disturb the peace of Great Horton Road? Maybe in our heads we were having a bright, noisy, racketing, roistering, hell-raising night of it, but we were just three unremarkable youths, who maybe seemed to be giggling inappropriately.

Gordon's background was similar to mine. His father liked a drink. The uses and abuses of alcohol were not so new to him. For Dave though, it was all new. His formidable forensic skills were just coming to the fore. He was used to exercising them analysing passages from Shakespeare and the work of the metaphysical poets. He used them now to analyse what was going on in his mind, how the drink was affecting him. It brought a new and noble dimension to the evening - now we were in the tradition of Frankenstein, or Dr Jekyll, or Sherlock Holmes, experimenting, inventing, creating, on the frontiers of science, dabbling with new and dangerous substances. We had a pint in the Kings, and then crossed the road to the Bull's Head to begin the return journey.

Four pints inside us and we had lift off. Our heads were among the stars and our feet walking on air. The Four Ashes arrived next, at the bottom of a dark forecourt. It was straight from the Bradford of gas lights and trams. Three fresh-faced lads bringing in the cold and high spirits must have been a novelty to the faded topers who lingered there. Flag floors, brown benches, cream walls flexed in and out of focus, only lightly sketched in compared to the huge pints that frothed before us.

The toilets were at the back, outside, open to the elements. There we were the three of us, peeing and giggling, Dave still trying to describe his changed perceptions - and then the snow came down, and that was it - the moment.

The snow spiralled down out of the blackness. It swirled about us, and as you looked up, it seemed it was we who ascended. The snow came even here. Even drunkards splashing in a trough of stinking urine could be blessed by its touch.

We left our wayward footsteps in the snow all the way to the White Horse for last orders, the last pint, the one that would separate the men from the boys. Now each mouthful had to be calculated. Each swallow could precipitate vomiting. Sometimes we got fish and chips over the road. 'It'll settle your stomach,' Gordon insisted. 'Once and for all,' I thought, but you couldn't be seen to be jibbing.

We parted company shortly after, Gordon and Dave taking Moore Avenue for Wibsey, for me Horton Bank beckoned. And still the snow came down.

Haworth in the Snow

It couldn't happen now, well not during daylight hours anyway, and who knows what legions haunt Haworth's main street after dark? During the daytime however it's always crowded. The crowds ebbing down mingle with crowd flowing up, and there are little eddies around the entrances to shops and cafes. Once though I was the only person on Haworth's main street. My walking companion Dave had gone in search of a shop. The snow was coming down, already it lay thickly, but there was not a footprint in it, only mine and they were filling fast.

Our Ogden Moor outings had often brought us to the Bronte borderlands. A bold striking out westward from Fly Flatts would land you on the Oxenhope - Hebden Bridge road, and beyond that it's Heathcliffe territory. It would take the best part of the day to get there though, so Bronte country was best explored by getting the bus from Chester Street in Bradford straight to Haworth.

I had a relative in Haworth, Great Aunt Mabel. I remember visits. The house was clean and cold. The fire-place had newspaper in the grate. There was newspaper on the floor to protect the carpet. Newspaper protected the furniture. As a child I was instructed to sit on a straight-backed chair and keep quiet. Children were no novelty in those days. No fuss was made of them. The atmosphere on one of Neptune's moons was probably more hospitable. When I think of her now, I'm reminded of Charles Dickens's Miss Murdstone.

It was after walking Haworth Moors that I first read the Brontes. The romance of their unfinished lives resonated with me. I yearned for some mystical encounter with the souls of just such young women. They however would have been much more at home with Great Aunt Mabel.

And indeed none of those High Tory Bronte girls would have had much to say to the dreamy, atheistic son of a mechanic, who had been educated beyond his station, but knowing they had trodden these moorland paths lent drama to what otherwise would have been a drear and barren landscape.

And so there I was, and that was the moment - me alone in the Main Street of Haworth with the snow descending. There must have been moments in years gone by when tiny boots had skipped through the snow, the hems of long garments becoming ice-balled; moments when cheeks had been flushed with exertion and excitement, and gloved hands had moulded tiny snowballs. Moments too when snow-light had brought luminosity to the still, cold cheek of someone lying at rest there in the Parsonage; moments when ...

A shop bell broke the spell and Dave emerged munching a Mars bar.

What Haworth has become would dismay the Brontes. They who had been so private, so reserved, would be horrified to see their lives laid bare, pinned out in display cases for all to see. Emily who loved the remoteness and solitude of their moorland home would be aghast to see the crowds pouring in at weekends and Bank Holidays. All those people coming from all parts of the globe drawn by the Bronte story. Of course most are there because Haworth is now on the tourists' itinerary along with London and Stratford and York. Few are interested in the Brontes and never have, nor never will, read a word they've written.

Dave and I had often followed the well-trodden way up to Top Withens on days of wind and rain, and even on days of sun and rain, but never on a day like this. It wasn't well-trodden on this day - no foot-prints to tread, only the tracks of sheep, whose ragged ice-bejewelled fleeces looked quite black beneath the covering of snow.

It had been freezing for days and beneath the snow was ice. It was hard to keep your footing and every other minute one or the other of us was brought to earth with a bump. This was amusing or tedious depending on whether you were observing it or experiencing it.

It was folly to attempt the walk. It was an easy path to follow in good light, but by the time we were returning, it was growing dark and alternatives proliferated. Snow-white paths seemed to beckon here and there, their pristine surfaces inviting the violation of our boots. Maybe a shadow flitted ahead and guided us. Maybe Emily, who of all of them, would have forgotten her prejudices and responded to the romance in our adolescent hearts. Maybe she led us to the point of safety, from which we could see the orange lights of Keighley twinkling in the frosty air.

There was time for a couple of pints in the Fleece, before we finally descended the dark evening street and caught the bus to Bradford.

Christmas by Bus

The moment of midnight passed in Guiseley and it was Christmas Day. I was on the last bus from Leeds to Bradford, number 55, the one that went via Horsforth, Yeadon, Rawdon, John O'Groats, and the Orkneys, when the tide was out. It was the one that, just when you think it had all made all the detours it could and was at last heading for home, would turn of again in pursuit of somewhere obscure.

Not a good idea getting on board after a few pints of Tetley's bitter. I've had some moments pregnant with desperation on that bus, wondering how much pressure the human bladder can take, fist and feet clenched, willing every light to turn green, with a sheen of cold sweat on my brow. And when at last the bus has berthed in Chester Street, I've flown off and fled to the nearest quiet corner - no toilets open late at night - and stood and stood until the steaming stream behind me stretched right across the bus station.

And so this was Christmas. I tried to stare past my dark reflection into the night beyond, but there was nothing to focus on - all good folk were abed and dreaming of Christmas Day. I was nineteen and Christmas was a dream I'd grown out of, though there were Christmas presents in my bag from Penny and later that day I'd be having a traditional Christmas dinner at home. Family Christmases had been scaled down. No more trimming up; no more real Christmas trees, just a small artificial one on top of the TV; no more parties. Sutcliffe had died in 1964 and we never saw much of Audrey and Gillian after that. It had been the friendship between him and Dad that had kept it going. Mum and Audrey could never really be bothered.

I don't remember those Christmases well, don't remember what presents I got, or what presents I bought. But then to say it's such a special day I don't remember many of the 57 Christmases I've had. If you think of them as lights on a tree; most of them have gone out. One I remember, the last one at home

Dad gave me two bottles of Websters Green Label for breakfast, the pint ones. Drinking alcohol at that time was not uncommon then. I've known him have whisky in tea before going to work on the six till two shift, a hangover maybe from the day when alcohol was thought of as strength-giving, when it pervaded life more, when the water wasn't safe to drink, and tea and coffee were too expensive

Afterwards I walked up the Bank and called at Graham's and was given a tumbler of vodka by his Mum, I seemed to amuse her for some reason, whether it was my wit, or the lack of it, I was never quite sure.

The Hare and Hounds was full and convivial. Not all pubs opened at lunchtime on Christmas Day, those which did, did well. We had three pints. Graham's Dad came in just before the pub closed and bought us a couple more pints each. He was a quiet man. His wife once decided to see how long it would be before he spoke, if she said nothing to him. The rest of the day passed in silence.

Back home for Christmas dinner. I had a sherry, wine and more beer. Afterwards I sat in the chair and fell asleep. I awoke at eleven at night in a confused state. I had a bottle of beer and went to bed. My last Christmas Day at home.

Leeds still wore steel-capped boots and a donkey jacket when I went to college there in the 1960s. There were no wine bars, no smoked glass and chrome. No Costa Coffee, no Starbucks, no Harvey Nicks. Many pubs were unadorned drinking shops, not sure whether they wanted long-haired types as customers, and there were those who were sure they didn't and wouldn't serve you.

I arrived at the end of the 1960s, in the baggage train, listening wide-eyed to stories of those who'd come back from the 'front,' those who'd been to the Isle of Wight festival, those who'd been at the Grosvenor Square demo, those who'd taken acid. I went a little way down the hippie trail, - long hair, beard, and the fur waistcoat, formerly my Auntie Elsie's fur coat. For Dad seeing me in the waistcoat was the last straw, the tin lid. After months of arguing about the length of my hair, it was a step too far, the giddy limit. It soon became clear that the only sensible thing, the only possible thing, was for me to move out.

Richard Pitt from Selby was on the same course as me, and also looking for somewhere to live, so we decided to share. At the time Leeds was razing large areas of red-brick housing. Areas in the south and the west, of the city looked as though the Luftwaffe had returned and done a more thorough job. There was a cheap house at Burley. It was semi-derelict, in a sea of red brick and rubble. I thought we could manage there, but Richard saw sense and refused, and we ended up in an attic flat at Noster Hill in Beeston, pleasant enough, though it did snow in through the skylight and we'd have a covering of snow on the beds.

I had a record player, but no records. Richard had all Bob Dylan's albums up to 'Blonde on Blonde.' That's all he had.

That's all we played. Richard did his Vesta beef curries. I had tinned pilchards and teacakes. Elland Road was nearby, the home of Leeds United. The late 1960s was a good time for the club - Leeds and Liverpool dominated the league as Manchester and Arsenal were to do 30 years later. In 1969 they were League champions They had a big skinhead following. If you weren't careful, you could get caught up in a crowd of them on match days. 'Oh he is a hippy bastard, yes he is,' they would sing jauntily, following me into town.

The Victoria Hotel behind the Town Hall was a pub that was happy to include students among its clientele, even though we'd often sit there all night nursing half a pint and sharing cigarettes. There was an alcove by the juke box where we congregated. On this Christmas Eve, there hadn't been many students about. Most had gone back home. I was going home too after seeing Penny. Richard had gone back to Selby. The flat was empty and uninviting.

Penny lived in Horsforth, on the number 55 route, so we got the last bus together. Quite a crowd when we set off, but it emptied as it distributed its passengers across the Leeds/Bradford hinterland. I'd caught it once and been left alone on the top deck with two young thugs who were indulging in some violent skylarking at the front of the bus. Inevitably they grew bored with that and turned their attention to me. They reeled down the bus and swung into the seat in front of me. Two pairs of blood shot eyes struggled to focus. The bigger of the two offered me the choice of fighting him on the bus, or getting off in Shipley and fighting there.

It was a tough decision. I felt inclined to postpone the encounter on the grounds that something might turn up. And it did. In the way drunks have their mood swung round and they decided I was a great guy. We became fast friends and shook hands vigorously a number of time to prove it. Before they got off in Shipley, the big guy showed me the knife he'd kept concealed in his jacket. It was a carving knife and he'd filed teeth down one side. I was glad we'd decided to be friends.

No such problems tonight. People got off in Shipley and I was the only one left on as we trundled through the empty streets towards Bradford. We went down Manningham Lane, past the spot where, many years earlier, I'd gazed in delight at Busby's display of toy soldiers. All the shops were in darkness now. Their tills had ceased ringing. Their Christmas rush was over for another year.

The bus slipped into its berth in Chester Street Bus Station and the engine fell silent. I came down the stairs. The driver was counting his money. He glanced up and clearly felt the need, despite himself, to acknowledge the season.

'Merry Christmas,' he said without conviction.

'Merry Christmas,' I replied.

Something flickered into life briefly, something timeless, something irrepressible. Even here it was Christmas, even here on the platform of a bus in the corner of a bus station, and we could no more deny it than Scrooge could say 'Humbug,' in the presence of the Ghost of Christmas Past.

I got off the bus and began the two mile walk home.

The Open Road

What you do is go to a big, well-known, motorcar showrooms and buy a car with a six or twelve month warranty, so that you'll be able to iron out all the faults before the warranty expires - right?

Wrong!

It's what I did though - went to one of Blackburn's premier motor retailers, used my skill and judgment to select an opalescent blue Austin Allegro with a black vinyl roof. I declined a test drive, knowing I'd be too pre-occupied driving an unfamiliar car to notice anything else, unless the wheels dropped off.

I checked the engine - there was one. I snooped round the car, even half-stooping to look for hidden rust. I sat in the driver's seat and perused the instruments. I pronounced myself satisfied. Indeed I could see myself cutting rather a figure, emerging from my dashing Allegro on the staff car-park at the library. I counted out the money. The salesman seemed rather disappointed; I suppose they prefer a challenge, or at least a show of resistance.

The problem with these places is that the buck is passed from hand to hand. The salesman may have a shrewd idea about the state of the car, but unless the mechanic has challenged him: 'I bet you can't find a sucker for this one,' he won't really know. And when you take it back to have problems sorted, you see a receptionist, not the mechanic, or rather the cack-handed, but willing lad, who's actually worked on your car.

The warranty period was exhausted dealing with the misfiring carburettor. You do need to be forceful to get things done properly. Stanley Bradley, a friend of mine who lived in nearby Prospect Terrace, when I was at Sunnyhurst in Darwen, said he'd threatened to drive a car through the showroom window before now, if he didn't get satisfaction. Also some mechanical knowledge helps. To this day I don't know what a carburettor is or does.

The more serious problem of the condition of the engine didn't emerge until after the warranty had expired, though I had been concerned at the blue clouds that appeared in the driving mirror whenever I started up in the morning, and at the pints of oil that had to be poured in every week. And it was a bad starter. On any but the sunniest days you approached it, not knowing whether it would fire up or not. I got into the habit of parking on a slope, so I could bump-start it.

No, if you want a car, go to a small garage where they do repairs and servicing, where the guy who sells you the car owns the place and does the work on the cars himself. He'll want to keep his customers happy. He wants them to give him a good name and come back. Big garages have so many customers, they can afford to lose a percentage.

It was Dave Wilson, whose wife Geraldine worked with me at the library, who introduced me to Jim. He'd been going to him ever since he'd learned to drive, and his father had been going there before him. Jim had a garage in Back Bonsall Street in Mill Hill in Blackburn, right next to the railway line. It wasn't somewhere you'd stumble upon by accident. Jim's father had been a farmer on the Woodfold Estate in Mellor, and Jim had been brought up to farming, but it was a precarious business and his father had sent him out to learn a trade, to become a motor mechanic.

There was still something of the farmer about him: weathered features and a rustic way of talking. I took the Allegro round and asked him what he thought.

'Properly speaking, it needs a new engine,' was his verdict.

So that's what it got, well a reconditioned one. I kept the Allegro a bit longer, but we never got on. We had not bonded in adversity. I asked Jim to let me know if he got anything in I might like. He came up with a lime-green Capri Ghia, also with a black vinyl roof. Not quite British racing green, but there was something about it - something redolent of a golden age of motoring, when the roads were empty, and you could roar past plodding farm carts with white dust boiling in your wake. It was only a Ford Cortina in wolf's clothing, a poor man's E-type, but it seemed to be a car that would take me places, down-town, up-town, glossy ad places, full of glamorous people.

It didn't do that, but it took us to Southampton a good number of times. Capri's were big on the outside and small on the inside, especially in the back, but that was OK for small children, as William and Emily were then. I'd found an attractive route via Marlborough and Andover and I remember a sunny evening rolling through the lengthening shadows of Savernake Forest, and along by Tidcombe Down with Beethoven's Sixth on the cassette player.

It was the first car I bonded with, identified with. It had been ten years old when I got it in 1986. I kept it for five years. It had a good, solid feel, like the cars of a former age that were built to last a lifetime. And yet it suffered from my benign neglect and slowly deteriorated. It had to go at last. It sat in Jim's yard for many a month, it's vinyl roof peeling, settling further into its bed of weeds and rust.

A Talbot Alpine next. It was a bit bashed in on one side, so I got it for £400 as it stood. It was a top-of-the-range model though, with power-steering, five gears and an automatic sun-roof, but it was only ever just a car.

Run of the mill cars followed: a Datsun Cherry, a Ford Escort, a Ford Fiesta, a Ford Sierra, a Ciroen BX, the only car I thoroughly disliked. It wasn't until I got the Toyota Camry in the year 2000 that I had any positive feeling about a car again.

The roads had been getting busier. They widened the M6 to four lanes. They carried the M65 through to Preston, but the roads still got busier. By the beginning of the twenty- first century there were few quiet times on the roads. Sundays, which had been the traditional day for new drivers to get a bit of practice, were busy. Staying at Linda's in Bedford once I set off back at eight in the evening, thinking it would be quiet, but the M6 was just as busy; juggernauts thundering along nose-to-tail through the night, just as they did through the day.

As I got older it seemed every time I went out in the car somebody did something to aggravate me. If I gave myself a safety margin, other drivers used it. If I left a safe distance between myself and the car in front, somebody would occupy it. If I drove at a sensible speed, somebody would pull out in front and make me brake. If I stuck to speed limits, I always had someone's windscreen in my driving mirror and could sense their irritation burning into the back of my neck. And people would overtake with bends approaching. How did they know nobody was doing the same thing coming the other way? Did they have radar? Were they just gambling, or were their reactions quicker, their judgement finer than mine?

It annoyed me when people overtook, even when it was safe for them to do so. It seemed like my driving was being criticised. It annoyed me when people overtook on motorways and then immediately braked as their exit loomed. Why didn't they pull in behind me? It annoyed me when people parked on narrow roads directly opposite a parked vehicle. It annoyed me when people stopped and threw open their doors, without looking to see if it was safe. It annoyed me when people threw rubbish and cigarette ends out the window. It annoyed me when people didn't indicate. It annoyed me when young people played their thud-thud racket at deafening levels. Sports utility vehicles annoyed me – those ugly, muscle-bound, planet-polluting, four wheel drive monsters that became fashionable in the early years of the 21st century. Ironically people bought them to be immune from the worst the weather could throw at them, and yet it was these gas-guzzling behemoths that were causing climate change and extreme weather. Lots of things were beginning to annoy me. I was getting old and the pace of life was getting too much for me.

The Toyota Camry was automatic. I'd never fancied an automatic, thinking it was just one more thing to go wrong, and rather liking the macho thing about changing gear. Jim persuaded me, saying it had a good engine and had been well looked after. I re-examined my prejudice against automatics and decided to try it.

The Japanese know how to make cars. The Datsun Cherry had been sound enough mechanically, it had just crumbled away, like an ancient corpse exposed to the sun. Driving the Toyota was comfortable and comforting. There was nothing to do but stop and start. It cruised along. The steering was almost telepathic. The thing knew where you wanted to go. It felt good going along really slowly and it felt good when you speeded up, which it did without any fuss. You could go a long, long way in it without getting tired, and I did - France a couple of times, and Scotland many times.

It never faltered, for five years it never faltered, and then at last in the car-park near Windermere in Ambleside, when I was with Linda and Andy and the kids, it refused to start. It was a shock. It was like a faithful old butler refusing to go down to the wine cellar to get you another bottle, saying you'd already had more than enough.

It had let me down, but maybe it had sensed something. Maybe it knew that it was about to be superseded. It was August 2005 and I was buying a van, a VW Transporter. Jim was getting it ready. I was going to convert it into a camper and I was heading for the open road.

Man's Best Friend

Strange to think now, but back in the 1950s it was quite normal for dog owners to turn their pet out first thing in the morning, leave it to wander all day, and not let it in until the evening, when it exchanged places with the cat.

It was normal to see dogs, solitary, or in ones and twos, on the street, something you would never see today. Fierce dogs were just another street hazard to contend with when you were young.

I'm told though that as a tiny child I used to toddle up to Billy, a fierce white bull terrier that lived near Auntie Elsie's, and run my finger along its teeth when it bared them at me. I suppose most sane dogs permit the very young to take liberties.

The first pet we had though was a ginger tomcat called Rufty. It didn't permit liberties, hence its name and the scratches on my hands and legs. It was Rufty who moved with us to 930 Great Horton Road and was so terrified of something on our first night there.

Our first dog was a sturdy little mongrel called Sherry. Dad was a regular at the Hare and Hounds at the top of Horton Bank. They had stables and a steady supply of puppies and kittens. When Dad had had a few, it was a simple matter to persuade him to take one home, tucked away inside his coat.

Sherry got run over and killed on Windermere Road. A Golden Retriever, Trixie, came next, but he bit me and had to go back. Then came Whisky. Whisky wasn't from the Hare and Hounds. There was a pet stall in the open air market in Bradford. Furry bundles of misery - puppies, kittens, rabbits were on display in cages. One bundle caught my eye for some reason - Whisky.

Whisky was 90 % collie, black and white, with a silky coat. Nature always does its best with mongrels, tries to produce a handsome beast with whatever genetic material it has to hand, but Whisky's proportions were not quite right - taken separately; head, body, legs they were fine, but together... Well she might never have won at Crufts, but she was the best dog in the world to me.

Her temperament was a little suspect. She was OK with us, unless she had a bone, and sometimes when I had play fights with her, I could see in her eyes she was getting close to letting rip. With strangers though, and particularly kennel owners she was a bad'un. More than once we returned from holiday to be told they wouldn't have her again. And indeed she did sneak out of her kennel as lithe and snarly as a panther, until she recognised us and would be transformed, leaping up in joy, and even licking the bandaged hand of the kennel owner.

Any supermarket today has a whole aisle devoted to pet food - special preparations for puppies, for old dogs, for big dogs, and small ones. There's gourmet pet-food for cats, dainty morsels for kittens. In the 1950s there was Lassie for dogs and Kit-e-Kat for cats, and our pets would do well if they ever got a tin of either. They had to make do with leftovers with, occasionally, bits from the fish monger or bones from the butcher

I did take Whisky for walks, but sometimes she was just let out on her own. She must have been in season once. She got pregnant. I didn't know, hadn't spotted that she was getting fat, hadn't been told, but one Sunday evening in September with the threat of school next day looming large, I heard strange squeaks from Whisky's lair in the cellar. I went to investigate and was amazed and filled with joy to see puppies squirming around her. Not since the day I got the toy soldiers had a dreary evening been so transformed.

There were four of them, two dogs, two bitches. Years later I found out there had been six, but Dad had drowned two, thinking it would be hard enough to find homes for four. Of course I wanted to keep at least one, preferably the bonnie little chap with the snow-white ruff, but it was out of the question. They had to go. I think Whisky was glad to see the back of them too. She was a reluctant mother. She never got caught again.

Whisky was the last dog we had while I was at home. When I left, Mum and Dad got an animal rescue dog, Shandy, who bore a sketchy resemblance to an Alsatian. She was amiable enough, fond of catching flies and easy to fool into thinking there was one there when there wasn't.

Although they complained about dog hairs and being haunted for food, Mum and Dad got a lot out of dogs. They reduced friction, channelled anger and permitted expressions of affection. They kept cats too, but didn't make a fuss of them. Cats were too stand-offish for them.

Penny and I got a couple of cats when we lived at Billinge Side, Sam and Snitch, two toms who couldn't stand the sight of each other. When Penny gave up work to have Jonathan, we got a puppy too, Bess, a Staffordshire Bull Terrier bitch from the County pub, which used to be at the top of Darwen Street in Blackburn. Maybe pets performed some of the functions for me and Penny that they had done for Mum and Dad.

Bess's bonhomie spread far and wide but it was only shallow. With dogs like Whisky attachments are deep and immutable. Bess loved anybody and everybody, but had a particular fondness for drunks and tramps. She showed no aggression, not even with other dogs, but her sheer ebullience could floor children and her tail was like whip-lash. Many a time baby Jonathan in his recliner felt the force of it across his startled face. When Penny and I parted, I felt it was unfair for Bess to be in the house all day on her own, so put an ad in the paper and sold her. When she went with her new owner, she didn't look back.

Sam had disappeared soon after we'd moved to Darwen. Snitch persevered and was even there when I got home after being in hospital for three weeks. He went too though in the end.

Pet owning became less widespread towards the end of the twentieth century. It had become more of a responsibility, letting dogs roam was no longer an option. People had nice homes, and dogs and cats soon ruin furniture and furnishings. People were more fastidious about fleas. More people had allergies to pet fur. Those who did have pets though lavished more care on them than previous generations had done on their children.

Getting Sandy was Fiona's idea. We'd had an unfortunate experience with Maxie, a border collie pup who hadn't seen herself at the bottom of the pecking order and had bitten Emily, so I wasn't keen on another dog. Sandy was an animal rescue puppy whose pregnant mother had been left by travellers. The dog warden had caught her when she had puppies in a rabbit warren. He got the mother and five puppies. That night it occurred to him that he might not have got all of them, so he went back the next day and watched the rabbit hole. After a while Sandy's face appeared. He managed to grab her.

Maybe she should have been called Lucky, maybe not. When Fiona left she took Sandy. Her new partner didn't really want her, and later Sandy came back. Insecurity seemed to be part of her make-up, but she had that deep attachment that reminded me of Whisky. She had a deep attachment too to her habits. At Cyprus Street she used to sleep upstairs in William's room and when it got to 8.00, she'd stand by the door wanting to be let upstairs. At Hollands Cottage she slept behind the sofa and by 8.00 she'd go there and would only reluctantly emerge, even when there was a bright fire burning. Though the rustle of a bag of Seabrook crisps would winkle her out.

Whisky had been fond of buses and would jump aboard if one stopped nearby. Sandy was a car dog. She approved of the the van. It gave her a better view, and she liked to sit in it when it was parked in the drive. The open road beckoned for her, just as it did for me.

My Darwen Library

They did things differently in Darwen; libraries for example. Darwen got off to a flyer, being the first non-borough to adopt the Public Library Act in 1871. Darwen Library was one of the first to allow the public access to books, which it did in 1896. In most libraries you had to ask at the counter and the librarian would go and see if the book was in. Darwen was a Liberal, non-conformist town and the Library Committee took its responsibilities seriously - no popular fiction for its readers. In Blackburn by contrast, a Tory, Church of England town, you could read what you wanted.

In 1908 Darwen got a new library with help from philanthropist Andrew Carnegie. Nothing happened for 66 years and then the reorganisation of local government merged Darwen with hated Blackburn, and the library became part of the Lancashire County Library Service. Librarian Arnold Holden had to move to Blackburn to be deputy there and a new Senior Librarian was appointed for Darwen; a striking, tawny blonde, Stella Barclay, who reputedly was more passionate about horses than books.

This is what I came into in January 1977. I didn't want to go and I wasn't particularly wanted, but a reorganisation at Blackburn forced me out. At Blackburn I was specialist reference staff; at Darwen I would be expected to do a bit of everything, and there were a lot of everythings I couldn't do. I'd never done counter-work, never done inter-library loan work, never even put a jacket on a book. I was a new boy again, but even worse, a new boy who knew it all, and thought what he didn't know wasn't worth knowing. It could have been a disaster, but Darwen was blessed.

Arnold Holden had been a knowledgeable bookman. It had a good book-stock. In the basement there were biographies of everyone, and town histories of everywhere, as well as standard works of literature and novels in major Eurpean languages, but its greatest asset was not its stock, but its staff. There was a body of good, experienced, warm-hearted, staff: Mary Grogan, Marie Heys, Dorothy Cordall, Diane Rigby, and later, Mary Painter. All of them could see through my superior airs and were big enough to overlook them. Mary Grogan in particular took care of me, took great pains to make me feel at home.

Stella's attention *was* divided, but the non-equine percentage, small as it was, was more than enough. She could think on her feet, see to the heart of the problem, and could charm anybody from dustbin men to dignitaries. She was happy to leave me to just get on with it.

The need to supply popular fiction at Darwen had been conceded years ago. Libraries were judged by their issue figures, and it was romances, westerns, crime and horror that flew off the shelves. The years of cut-backs and closures were looming; libraries could not relax, assured that they were self-evidently a good thing. They had to justify themselves. The evolutionary change, the revolution that was to make libraries unrecognisable to a nineteenth century user was beginning.

Recorded music caused librarians headaches - should it be made available? At first only classical music was bought, and then jazz and folk, and then, after years of agonising, popular music. I was sent once to Reidys Music Shop in Blackburn to buy several hundred pounds worth of LPs. Punkish youths idling there voiced their derision as I amassed a pile of stuff, which they thought was all for me. As such a valued customer the staff brought me a cup of coffee.

It took a long while, but I assumed a pivotal role at Darwen. I could fire up the boiler. I could operate the stage lighting in the theatre I could do the caretakers' timesheets I could work out the bills for bookings for rooms I could interview prospective staff I could do research queries I could do bibliographic checking I could work on the counter I could work on the enquiry desk. I could select stock. I could withdraw stock, though didn't do much of the latter - I preferred to relocate items to the basement - just in case. I even knew how to check the top-secret equipment that would give warning of a nuclear strike. It was located in the... well I'd better not say where.

I came to identify with Darwen Library. I came to see it as an endangered species, threatened both by neighbouring Blackburn and, more remotely, by Lancashire County at Preston.

I stayed there seven years, which was far too long. I should have stayed a couple of years, and then used Darwen as a launch-pad to a glittering career. Maybe there are people who plan their future, who know exactly where they'll be ten years from now, but most just blunder into jobs, just happen to be in the right place at the right time, when some kind of reorganisation takes place, or a vacancy arises.

Darwen had been a retreat from the world of information technology. They still used the Browne issue system, still used tickets and charging-cards, filed in various sequences in trays on the counter. In those days the library was very busy. On Saturdays the queues stretched right through the revolving doors and into the street. Staff became adept at holding a pile of books open with one hand, reaching through gaps between colleagues to search the issue, all the while conducting a cheerful conversation with the borrower. The pile of tickets to be filed grew and grew and even the most nimble-fingered assistant couldn't keep up. Computers promised to put an end to all that.

And of course they did, but the first system was basic and prone to break-downs. It wasn't unknown for staff to pretend it was working, the alternative being to write down a twelve digit number for each book and in-put them manually later. Computers as information sources were a long way off. Books were still the thing.

I nurtured both the local and reference collections, liberating the local collection from the glass cupboards that had confined it, and giving it a place on the shelves that reflected its growing importance. Family history was still a marginal activity then, indulged in only by reduced aristocrats.

And then 1983 dawned; the year I did things, the year I learned to ride a motor bike and went on a camping holiday in Scotland. It was the year I went on a writing course at Lumb Bank near Hebden Bridge, where I met my second wife, Fiona, and it was the year I started looking for other jobs. I'd never whole-heartedly embraced librarianship, never become a member of the professional association. Was I thinking I was somehow keeping my options open, not committing myself? Was it me just not wanting to join things? Whatever, a result of it was that my choices were limited. Many jobs were available only to chartered librarians; librarians who'd been members of the Library Association for two years. So, despite being in my mid-thirties, I was still applying for junior jobs.

One came up at Whalley - running the branch, and the two mobiles that operated out of there. It seemed ideal, idyllic almost, a complete change from industrial Darwen and Blackburn. There were two of us in for it, the other candidate had worked at Whalley for many years and considered himself the rightful heir. County Librarian Mike Dolan chaired the interview, along with Ribble Valley Librarian Barbara Snell and her deputy Sue Holden.

Normally the result was known a few hours after the interview; days went by and still there was no announcement.

Kippford

I once saw a falcon recalibrating its sights over the motorway verge and, although it was a grey and rain-peppered day, there seemed to be sunlight on its plumage. It reminded me of Scotland, where the rainy days are illuminated somehow. A light leaks from somewhere - from the past, from another Scotland where the sun always shines?

It's this that draws you back, draws me anyway- this promise of somewhere different, somewhere better - somewhere beyond the silver horizon, somewhere over the shining water. It's this that makes you stuff the car-boot with woollies, wellies and wind-cheaters and join the M6 traffic heading north. I always prefer to head north: heading south means congestion, claustrophobia, and the ultimate chaos of London; north means open spaces, quiet roads, air you can breathe.

A lot of the traffic exits for Blackpool; then for Lancaster,

Kendal, Keswick, Carlisle, but there's plenty left after the M6 ends, enough to make queues on the A74. Gretna Green offers a diversion. All things Scotch are here. Here are tartan scarves, socks, ties, mugs, badges. Here is haggis, shortbread, Edinburgh rock, salmon, kippers, Highland cheeses, Highland music: the skirling of the pipes for newly married couples.

This version of Scotland was a Victorian invention, like Christmas. The real Scotland is different: long towns; low cottages; wet, seagull-haunted quaysides - stone harbours, where the sea endlessly chases its tail, jostling the sun-bleached boats. And the wind, always the wind

Any direction from Gretna Green but south is good, hard to resist the call to go west though. You can bypass Dumfries now, but once you had to go through the town. There'd be hold-ups, but also the chance to contemplate the rosy-granite buildings and the burnished silver claymore of the river. What lies beyond Dumfries is worth waiting for anyway.

When I was married and William and Emily were young, we used to come this way to a caravan site at Kippford. We'd have long weekends. We came maybe half a dozen times. It was like having a holiday home. After you reported to reception, the lady would get on her bike and lead you to your caravan. It was a hillside site, with the caravans on different levels, all having some kind of view. That was always a good moment, the one just after you'd arrived, sitting there with a cup of tea, looking at the view.

We went once with sister-in-law Sara and her husband Roy. It added something to the holiday; an echo of the time long ago when Sutcliffe and his family came on holiday to Cayton Bay. There was something else too: we were introducing them to Scotland, to a favourite place. We were in two cars; I was on my own in my red Ford Escort leading the way with the luggage, everybody else was behind in Roy's big Rover.

I didn't see how they could fail to be impressed, but decided to take the Solway Coastal route, just to make sure. It was late afternoon in late May and the sun was shining. It couldn't have been better. The road was deserted, and there was the sea - deeper blue than the sky, it shimmered, overlaid with gold, and something of that gold was in the very air. It dusted the fells of Lakeland beyond the Firth. And, before you could begin to take it in, really appreciate it, it was snatched away, as the road turned, and there'd be hedgerows and green fields there instead. Further on there'd be further glimpses - beaches where the sun dazzled on the wet sand and coves where black rocks stood firm against the seething foam. I felt sure they were all in raptures behind, but maybe they weren't, maybe the kids were fighting and the others absorbed in family gossip.

I put my foot down and got ahead so I could be unpacked and have a welcoming cup of tea ready. Sara and Roy usually holidayed abroad. I was showing them what delights they were overlooking.

Later we walked down the lane to the river. There was a bungalow for sale, a corner bungalow with a large garden. We wondered what it would cost and what it would be like to live there.

Kippford Yacht Club is down by the river and there are some pretty impressive boats there. Imagine having the bungalow and one of them - imagine being able to sail away, sail away to Morecambe, to Ireland, to Spain, to the West Indies and, more excitingly, being able to sail back and moor within sight of your home.

I'd often dreamt of owning a yacht and the dream had resurfaced resurfaced quite recently when I was thinking about retirement. I saw myself as a game and grizzled skipper, piloting a trim craft round the Med, exploring Greek isles and their history; with summer voyages to the Western Isles, maybe putting in at places like Kippford and thinking what a landlubber I had been. But then I read a book about yachting and how difficult it was to be sure of landmarks. Knowing how easily I can get lost, even on way-marked woodland trails, knowing too how navigation calls for meticulous calculation, and having failed O level maths three times, I decided a life at sea wasn't for me.

The daylight was ebbing. Only out on the Solway Firth was the sun still bright on the water. We went into the Anchor Hotel for a drink and a meal. It was busy and hot with red faces, clattering cutlery, clashing plates, food smells and jolly chatter. The kind of place where you need a few pints inside you to make the crowd and the noise recede a bit.

Later I sneaked out with my Guinness and sat on the wall by the river. It was warm enough to be out without a coat - just. The sky was dark, with a few lighter tones to mark the departing day. Now was the moment, now, as the planet turned and the sea felt the tug of the moon.

The others emerged from the bright pub to join me and I could tell by their hushed tones that they too were touched by the spirit of the place - even the kids scampered softly up and down and shouted in whispers. It was a rare moment.

Magic Buses

The trams might have gone long since, but not for Jim Halsall, Blackburn's transport and tram historian; when he stepped out of his front door in Blackburn's Higher Audley district, he could still see a Siemens class 36-75 car battling up Eanam brow on its way to the depot at Intack. When he dozed by the fire at night and his hand twitched, he was on the Queens Park route at the controls of one of the United Electric Combination trams with its Brill 22E traction bogies, one of the 76-81 class with the dwarf trolley masts.

I was too late for trams, though I did travel on them as an infant in Bradford, and I have dim memories of the Leeds ones. It was buses for me and although I was never a bus enthusiast in the way Jim was a tram enthusiast, they were a big part of my growing up. Bradford Corporation buses were blue and cream; Halifax's were orange and lime-green and cream. The West Yorkshire ones were bright red. There were dark red Hebble buses and dark blue Sammy Ledgard ones. I liked travelling by bus. They were exciting. They could take you on a magical mystery tour, but did I really want to be on one for the best part of a day and a half?

Two bus journeys separated by over 40 years. Such different circumstances, such different times, hard to believe it was the same person on each one, and it was not of course. You're not the same person from one moment to the next - it's just an illusion, some trickery of memory and momentum. If the fifteen year old boy could meet the 57 year old man - how they would stare at each other, how they would stammer - 'Was I you?' 'Are you what I become?' How disappointed both would be.

The first journey was in 1964.

As with everything else we lagged behind the Sutcliffes when it came to holidays. They had ITV before us. They had a car before us. They had Chinese food before us. They had cheese and onion crisps before us. Sutcliffe had a bar in his house before us and had it stocked with all kinds of exotic drinks - Tia Maria, Blue Bols, Green Chartreuse, Crème de Menthe, whilst we just had a couple of shelves in an alcove with bottles of Websters Green Label and Mackeson on them. And they went abroad before us - Spain, they went to Spain, and had the bullfight poster on the wall behind the bar to prove it, as well as several pairs of castanets and a donkey with a hat.

It was still Scarborough for us, whence we returned with lettered rock of every flavour and boxes of kippers. When I reached adolescence I became a graceless creature, trailing sulkily in the wake of Mum, Dad and Linda, for whom a family holiday was still a glory, albeit a fading one. Maybe it was an attempt to recapture some holiday excitement that triggered Dad's initiative, maybe it was his suppressed spirit of adventure breaking out again. He decided we were going abroad. Nothing so common as Spain. It was Austria for us, and the Sutcliffes were coming too; less chancy if we had some seasoned travellers with us.

How much we forget. This was a landmark event: my first time abroad, and, just as with so many Christmases, much is beyond recall. Is it all there? Are there memory cells somewhere that contain all the details? Are they there in some remote and rarely visited part of the brain, but potentially accessible, if the way there were known, if a path through the undergrowth could be hacked, and if the key could be persuaded to turn in the rusty lock? Then I'd remember. All would be as clear as a summer's morning.

Did we pick up our coach in Bradford or Halifax? Was it fine and sunny? Was the mood jolly or jittery? Mum would have been making the best of a bad job: 'All that way by bus,' she would have intoned dismally to Dad's annoyance. 'Don't worry. There'll be plenty of toilet stops,' he would have reassured her. No toilets on the buses then though; no tea on tap; no constant coffee; no music; no videos.

The bus took us to Ashford airport in Kent. We were flying across the channel, cue more dismal forebodings from Mum. We had a break in Northampton. In a cafe an old man spotting us for travellers and hearing where we were bound, advised us, on the strength of his own World War One experience, that the only language Europeans understood was the point of a bayonet. Encouraged by his advice, we resumed our journey.

Ashford airport was more like the airfields of the last war than the airport lounges of today. Major, modern airports are like shopping malls - the flight is just another consumer item. At Ashford there were fields, airstrips and a few huts, housing customs and cafe.

After a cup of tea we wandered out into the afternoon sunshine to our aircraft like a bomber crew about to fly a mission. Aeroplane buffs would be able to tell you what kind of plane awaited us. I can't but it did have propellers, and when they got going the din was terrifying. I wasn't to hear anything like that again till I started work in the mill. One image that isn't lost, and locked away in a disused memory cell, is of looking out along the wing and seeing it vibrating fit to shake out all the rivets. Sheep raced away in a field below getting smaller and smaller. I didn't look at Mum. Sutcliffe's face was glued to the window. He was grinning avidly.

The coach was waiting for us at Ostende. There were two stocky, jolly, Belgian drivers. Being abroad then was more foreign than it is now. The cars seemed exotic - you didn't see Renaults and BMWs and Fiats in England then. It was all Fords and Morrises and Austins. The food too was different. The wine and beer were different. You can get French and German produce in any English supermarket now, but not then.

I wanted to preserve this foreign adventure, make it permanent. I collected little packets of sugar and salt, books of matches, beermats - anything with evidence of being abroad on it: foreign words, foreign designs, foreign lettering. At Brussels there was the Atomium, left over from the World Fair of 1958, its shiny silver spheres showing over the rooftops

There was a stop for a meal before it got dark. How vivid was the sensation of being on foreign ground, seeing a foreign sunset, with foreign street lights coming on, illuminating the hoardings with their foreign slogans. In the fields were foreign cattle and foreign sheep.

The night gathered us up. We roared into it. There was a stop at the Dutch border, made longer when Mum asked to get out for the toilet and didn't emerge until we'd passed through the checkpoint. She was left to try and negotiate her way without passport or papers. Was it with some reluctance that Dad went back to retrieve her?

On through the night. It wasn't comfortable, although my young limbs were supple. I practised a little repertoire of positions, changing whenever the discomfort became too much. We roared on into the night.

Should you try to sleep, or stay awake? Not much to see out of the window, but your own reflection. Getting to sleep was difficult and you often felt worse after it. There were stops in the middle of the night for the toilet. Not everybody got off. Many remained huddled under coats. The drivers sometimes changed over without stopping the coach, one sliding into the seat beneath the other and taking control of wheel and pedals. On into the night, roaring down the autobahns of Germany. I fell asleep at last.

And it was when I awoke that the moment came, at dawn, when the world emerged from blackness. We were in the countryside. Everything was a cold, blue monochrome. On either side there were towering clouds veiled with mist, clouds that piled up and up, clouds with trees and waterfalls and little cuckoo clock houses . . .

Not clouds! They were not clouds. They were solid. We were in Bavaria and these were mountains. It was a shock, a revelation. I was suddenly wide awake.

Forty years later and there are four of us on the Boulevard, the bus station at Blackburn, the only ones there. It's early on a cold, Sunday morning in March. No there are three of us. Ringo has gone to look for a newsagent. It irritates me. I've told him there won't be one open, and his wandering off reminds me of Sutcliffe cutting things fine. The bus will turn up and he won't be here.

Catching buses had become a marginal activity by the beginning of the 21st century. When I arrived in Blackburn in the early 1970s there were still long queues at teatime and the buses in the morning were always full, but by the 1990s buses were mainly used by the elderly, children and the poor. Even long distance coach journeys were usually made by people on a budget, people who had plenty of time; the retired or the unemployed or students.

The other two with me are Gordon, a colleague of Ringo's at Calderstones Hospital and Mike, a colleague of mine from Blackburn Library. We're off on a Harry Shaw Holiday to Lake Garda, five days, four nights, half-board and a free bar - £140, only snag being it's by bus, a 27 hour journey.

In a way all four of us are semi-detached from the mainstream of things, on the margins. We wander up and down, hunched against the cold, with the detritus of the Saturday night blowing around us. We've opted out, or maybe just been left behind. We have jobs rather than careers, homes to live in rather than show off, and the joys of marriage belong only to Mike. For Ringo and me 2004 is the year when we're going to do more, get out of the rut. Already we've had a weekend in Amsterdam, and we've a battlefield tour of France and Belgium booked for May. I run out of steam after that, but Ringo goes on to Austria, Germany and China, Egypt and Cuba. But now it's Italy.

The bus is on time, sleek and blue and brand new. This is its maiden voyage and there are teething troubles with the door to prove it. Ringo has wandered back into view, gazes disinterestedly at the bus, climbs aboard and is allocated the best seat - the one with most leg-room, and next to the window. I get the worst one of course, hardly any leg room and next to the aisle, and me with my knee. And I was the one who booked the holiday, sorted out the insurance, did all the arranging. I don't say anything.

It's nearly empty. Glynis, the courier, is from Birmingham. She has tinsel in her braided hair. The coach swings this way and that out of still-sleeping Blackburn and on to the M65. Every now and then we pull over to the hard shoulder, so the driver can fiddle with the door. I'm sitting next to Mike. He has a bag of toffees. I've a book of detective stories. Gordon has a huge carrier bag full of roast chicken legs, ham sandwiches, tuna sandwiches, boiled eggs, samosas, fancy cakes, apple pies, sweets, nuts, crisps and fruit. Ringo has a bottle of vodka. We each fall to our own devices.

We get off the motorway to pick people up from various Manchester suburbs and satellite towns. The coach gets quite full. Even though the four of us are all in our 50s, we're the youngest on board. We get back on the motorway and, stops to fiddle with the door apart, thunder steadily southwards. There's a toilet on the bus and Glynis is happy to produce tea or coffee at any time. The seats are comfortable enough, but the motorway stops are welcome - chance to stretch legs; ease aching knee; marvel at the prices in the services; and mooch idly in the shelter of the bus while Ringo smokes a pipe. It's wet and cold all the way.

We detour to Harry Shaw's garage near Coventry, so the door can be sorted out and then on to London, Kent via the Dartford Tunnel, and Dover. The journey is unremarkable, accomplished without much fuss. I don't get much reading done what with chicken legs and toffees being offered back and forth, and Mike, always anxious lest I should miss something, elbowing me to point stuff out.

It's a bit choppy going over the Channel, enough to make you stagger and hold on, and nobody lingers on the top deck, the open deck. The lights of Calais are pretty much like the lights of Dover. Back on the bus, and then we're away on the long dark night that is France. I go through my repertoire of positions, but my joints aren't as supple as they were 40 years before. I wonder if I need the toilet, or can I manage to the next stop? Ringo proffers vodka and I wonder if I should seek oblivion, or will I just feel worse in the long run?

We stop for an evening meal and when we're back on board, Glynis lowers the lights and puts the video on. It's 'Mr Bean.' I ask Ringo to pass the vodka.

I wake up in Switzerland. It's light and there's snow up there on the chalet rooftops. Despite that it's warmer. The sun is a brighter, more genial fellow than its pale, elusive, English cousin. The bus has come to seem like our natural environment, like home - 24 hours gone and three more to go; we could have flown to Australia in less time.

Italy at last, and as we reach the lakes, Glynis begins to talk us through, making tantalising references to battles and incidents, the details of which elude her. We're heading for Riva at the north end of Lake Garda. The hotel is right at the front. We don't have long to get our cases out; the Mayor doesn't like to see the square cluttered with coaches.

There's a bit of a wait sorting out rooms. We're all tired and the road's still unwinding before our eyes. We get the keys at last. I open up the room, dump my bag on the nearest bed, walk over to the window, and it hits me.

The sky is blue. The lake is sparkling blue. There are orange trees and lemon trees and beyond, a mountain backdrop with snow.

I just stare. It's wonderful. The air coming in through the open window is warm, but shot through with the freshness of early spring. It's a moment that makes the previous 27 hours seem... well, not so bad.

Away in a Manger

It's something I say every year. It's one of the things people do say, like saying they've had a 'quiet Christmas:'

'Wouldn't it be nice to get completely away from it all at Christmas?'

What's envisaged is a remote cottage, besieged by snow; fridge and freezer well stuffed; well-stocked wine cellar; and a roaring log fire, with no pressure to try and visit all your family and friends; to be in two places at once; to be setting off on journeys in dodgy conditions; having to be careful not to have too much to drink the night before etc.

A fantasy of course, you can't do it any more than George Bailey could quit Bedford Falls and travel the world in 'It's a Wonderful Life.' More than that though, Christmas is all about home. It's a celebration of the home - home at its most inviting. You trim up. You decorate the tree. You spend money you haven't got on drinks and good things to eat, just so yours is the hearth everybody wants to sit around, yours the fire where everybody wants to roast their chestnuts, crack their walnuts, and admire the colour of their hot, smoking toddy against the flames.

Nevertheless I have spent a good few Christmases away from home.

There were Christmases in Southampton, about as far south as you can get on the mainland, but once there was snow. It descended gently. It was like haunting music. It dusted the roof tops like icing.

It's 250 miles from Darwen, a five hour journey if all goes well, and Fiona and I did it many times when William and Emily were little, and often in cars that, Capri Ghia apart, never ensured peace of mind. How often would I be anxiously watching the temperature gauge, listening to disturbing knocks and vibrations, while trying to keep peace in the back? In fact how many times did I listen to the temperature gauge, see disturbing knocks and vibrations, while trying to dissuade the kids from pouring their juice over one another, while all the time Fiona stared morosely out into the passing night?

It was always good to arrive; to get off the A35; to turn into Elmsleigh Gardens; to let Grandma take the kids away to get the chocolate out of their hair; to let Fiona unburden herself to her sisters; to let the car go off the boil; let the hissing die down; the steam evaporate; the glow of metalwork grow dull; to sit alone in the vast smart lounge with a cup of tea that I hadn't made myself; to watch unfamiliar local news on the vast, smart TV; and to know I'd nothing more to do for several days but be a shadowy figure in the background.

And there is something attractive about being an extra in somebody else's Christmas, not to have to think about meals, do shopping, plan festivities, to have nothing more to do than a bit of driving, some washing up, maybe asking what people want to drink. To be able to participate whole-heartedly, or pay the merest lip-service according to whim.

By the late 1980s the centre of Southampton had become a Mecca for shoppers and at Christmas was full of devoted worshippers. I avoided it if at all possible, but didn't mind Portswood in the suburbs. I didn't mind a jaunt down there to pick up a few things. We were there one Christmas Eve. It was bright and frosty. The shops were bustling, but not desperately so. All I needed was the Guardian and a bottle of vodka, but there were other things we had to get, finishing touches, trifling things: paper doilies, lametta, flowers, hundreds and thousands, marzipan angels, Christmas crackers.

Everybody was in good humour. The heavy work of Christmas shopping was over. People were getting odds and ends: a few more mince pies, some brandy for the pudding, another loaf - you can never have too much bread: the shops won't be open again for two days! An echo here I think of when you had to stock up for winter because things were not going to start growing again for another few months. After all Christmas is really the celebration of the winter solstice, when people killed their beasts and salted them down to see them through the worst of winter.

And it was when we were gathered by the window of a confectioner's that the snow began to fall. I hadn't noticed that the sky had changed, that the blue had gone and the sun become a pale disc in a feather-bed of grey down. Fine snow was flying on the wind, flocking and swooping like fairies doing aerobatics. Fiona and her sister and a few strangers were admiring the display of savouries and cakes and mince pies dusted with icing sugar in the confectioner's window. There were some doughty looking Stollen cakes, typically Germanic and formidable.

"They shouldn't be selling those, they're stolen," I said, the sally prompted by all the propitious signs of Christmas. Fiona pretended not to have heard. Her sister Sara gave me a sympathetic smile and a stranger - a handsome, matronly woman of seeming affluence smiled warmly at me.

And that was the moment - all of Christmas in prospect; the snow descending; a spark of communion with this other person, nothing to do that afternoon, but sit in the vast smart lounge and watch old black and white Christmas films, with the snow coming down outside and the kids subdued by the awe of Christmas, nothing to do but just wait for my vodka to chill nicely in the fridge. That was the moment.

Later Bedford, where Linda and Frances lived, became our Christmas destination. The M6 was the most direct route, but Birmingham's mass slowed traffic to a standstill, so I often took the M62 and the M1. Sheffield, Nottingham and other potential centres of gravity didn't arrest the flow of traffic quite so much. William and Emily were older, so less trouble, and there was even a time when we all liked the same kind of music and could complete the journey, as the sun was going down over the Bedfordshire fields, to tapes of sixties hits or the Beatles.

Frances, being still a child, bore the weight of our expectations then, all our hopes of Christmas magic rested on her. She obliged in so far as she could - she would insist on cake and sherry being left out for Father Christmas and bread for the reindeers, but she knew it was all a pleasant pretence. She knew where her presents came from, knew what they would be. Indeed she could not abide surprises – the tension, the suspense were too much. She had to know, and so we got into the way of letting her choose her present from us, going into Bedford and methodically combing the toyshops. Often this was on Christmas Eve, and going into town shopping on Christmas Eve, with no clear idea of what you want, is not a recipe for Christmas magic.

And yet you can walk into Bedford from Linda's, so no parking or traffic problems. The shopping centre is fairly compact, so decisions can be put on hold and you can always nip back for something you saw earlier, if nothing better materialises.

It was Christmas Eve and cold. It gets very cold in Bedford. So far from the benign influence of the winter sea, the cold can get a powerful grip, can strike the ground hard and force trees and plants to blossom with frost crystals. And the snow does come. Years may go by without it, but it comes at last, blown on the bitter east winds, the winds that have all the blizzard-breeding grounds of cruel, implacable Russia behind them. As someone once said 'there's nothing between Bedford and Siberia, but the spire of Cologne Cathedral,' and then the south-east grinds to a halt and those of us in the cosy north view the TV news pictures of snowbound traffic with complacency and think 'Thank God our baths are full of coal.'

No snow, but cold enough to be grateful for the warmth of shops and shopping malls, as Frances got to work. I am sometimes beguiled by the idea of shopping, sometimes sitting by the fireside I make lists and look forward to it, but the reality is I've no appetite for it, have no patience, no stamina, no resources. If I can't find what I want; if there are queues; if things are dearer than I thought, I give up. I go home empty-handed. Of course that's not an option if you're shopping with someone else, especially women, especially if they're shopping for clothes. And it's not an option either if you're shopping with a small child for a Christmas present on Christmas Eve.

Frances of course didn't bother to elicit my opinion, but Linda and Emily were consulted and William too if a computer game was being considered. Best not to comment if your opinion is sought, I always find. It is always ignored and only prolongs matters. You may start out feigning interest and pretending to be making judicious decisions, but a couple of hours later you'll be saying 'Yes it's fine, it's fabulous. Get it Get it! For God's sake get something!'

We scoured the toyshops, failed to find anything, and went back again to re-evaluate earlier prospects. The town was bustling, but not overwhelming. There was no feeling of desperation. And if the truth be known I didn't feel so bad. I was cocooned by the 'this isn't my Christmas. I'm not responsible' feeling. There was only this one present to buy and the short-list was getting shorter.

I declined to re-enter one of the shops and stood out on the street while the others went in. There was a Salvation Army brass band getting ready to play. On the nod they tucked heartily into 'God Rest Ye Merry Gentlemen.' It was a fruity, full-bodied rendition. It filled the street and brought a sudden harmony, an unexpected sense of occasion to the scene, as though we were all suddenly taking part in something, a movie, something moving anyway.

It was a transforming moment. I forgot the cold. I forgot the boredom, the incipient impatience. For a moment all my Christmases had telescoped together and I was at the heart of them.

The shop door opened. Linda put her head out. 'She's decided!' She announced. It was with a warmth and gladness I hadn't anticipated that I reached for my wallet.

Houlgate

We're in the queue for embarkation. It's hot. The sun dazzles on the waiting windscreens. During the First World War Granddad Lorenzo Darley would have been shouldering his kit and climbing the gangplank at Southampton Docks, with the Somme in prospect. In 1944 Uncle Stanley would have been manoeuvring his tank into a landing craft, with the Normandy beaches waiting. We're in line for the P&O ferry from Dover to Calais, bound for a Eurocamping holiday, but I feel sick, sick with apprehension at the prospect of driving abroad for the first time.

It's a Thursday afternoon late in May, at the very end of the twentieth century. There's Linda and Frances, William and Emily and me. We've a week at Houlgate in Normandy booked. It had been Linda's idea to go to France for a change; we usually went to Scotland. France was easier for her to get to than Scotland, as it was in Dr Johnson's day, when the Continent was more accessible than the Highlands. We'd discussed it at her house at Christmas, and as always when somebody proposes something that's months away, I'd agreed, thinking it might never happen.

The ferry comes in, towering over the P&O buildings. We continue to wait. Cars appear, racing down the ramp, glad to be back in dear old Blighty, and when the last of them has gone . . . Nothing. The wait goes on.

At last the column at the end begins to move. Car engines begin starting. This wouldn't be a good time for ignition failure. We're in my car, a maroon Sierra, not a car to get excited about, but it's been OK, reliable, but this is its first trip abroad, an irresistible opportunity for tantrums. It does start and I follow the car ahead. There's a sense of exhilaration - up over the iron ramps and into the lower decks. The loaders cram you in, gesticulating with great urgency, not satisfied until you're just where they want you to be, then you grab what you can out of the car and climb the iron steps up to the higher decks, where there are shops and bars and music, and excitable French children running this way and that.

The army record for 1834 Sapper Lorenzo Darley RE was blitzed in the last war. He died when I was fifteen and there's nobody alive now who knows what he went through. His wartime experiences are lost, unless they exist still - eternally, infernally being replayed, and can be visited one day. Mum said whenever he crossed over to France, he was sick. Today it's calm, but there's just that slight shimmer, that slight sense of being afloat, that disorientates. There's a video in the lounge area, but it's being played sotto voce. I can't concentrate anyway, the imminence of French roads distracts me.

The sea drives past, wave after wave, manically waving us on, the fathomless, indescribable sea. Huge as this rumbling, grumbling ferry is, it's nothing to the sea. The sea could engulf us and not know. The sea takes its cue from the sky. Where it is blue the sea is all blue dimples. Where there are white clouds the sea is white; grey where it's grey, muddy where it's muddy, but where the sun shines, it glitters like gold. Nothing on the sea today, but when

Uncle Stanley crossed there would have been vessels all the way to the horizon, and Granddad's troopship too would have had escorts.

France is sighted. Queues begin to form by the doors to the lower decks. France approaches - you can see houses, cars, people. France edges nearer. France arrives. We've docked. There's a lot of shouting and clanging of iron doors. The queue begins to shuffle forward and we descend to the waiting cars. Engines start up, including mine thankfully. Exhaust gases mist the air. Loaders begin to gesticulate frantically and we're away, up over the metal ramp, out into the bright sunlight of France. There are no custom formalities. We drive unregarded through the dock area and out on to the streets of Calais. I'm driving on French roads.

Linda's a good navigator, which is just as well, because when I looked at the map it was impenetrable; all the roads had two numbers. We're soon out of the town and bowling along quiet, smooth highways. The iconography of the road signs is very different, understated. It would be easy to miss a turning, but everything's OK. I haven't tried overtaking yet, but then everybody's whizzing past me.

There are 'aires,' or services every ten miles or so on the motorways. Some are just a picnic area with toilets and an emergency phone. We stop at one such and I sit on the grass in the warm sunshine, thinking this isn't so bad, in fact, not bad at all. Linda comes up looking concerned - the girls have locked themselves in the toilet and can't undo the bolt!

Behind the locked door Frances is wailing and Emily being brave, but with tears in her voice. Their combined efforts fail to budge the bolt. Linda and I exchange despairing glances. The toilets are arranged in a circle and open at the top. I walk round. There are some wash-basins. Standing on one I manage to haul myself up and clamber on to the top. I begin to crawl back round to the compartment where the girls are, much to the alarm of French ladies squatting below. My French is not up to explaining the situation; 'Pardon Madame,' will have to do. I drop down into the cubicle. It flashes through my mind that the situation will not be much improved if I can't free the bolt either. I can. We're out.

'Let's go before the Gendarmes get here,' I hiss.

If you were on a bus, or in the train, you'd feel the scenery was passing you by - driving, you feel part of it. The roads are empty and open. I overtake at last; a little tin truck with corrugated sides. The countryside is deserted. You drive through villages and hamlets where not a soul stirs. Buildings of antique brick stand in the roadside dust. Not even a cat stirs.

The Normandy Bridge crosses the Seine from Le Havre to Honfleur. It's not been there long. It opened in 1995 and is one of the longest, cable-stayed suspension bridges in the world. It's an uplifting experience and when you come down to earth again at the other side, you feel you've arrived somewhere different, in a distinctive region, with blue skies, blue sea and bright sunshine. The light has a different quality.

We drive through Trouville, along the Cote d'Emeraude, though Villiers-sur-Mer and arrive. We arrive at Houlgate, a small resort built in the nineteenth century when sea-bathing became popular. There's not much traffic, and I have to think carefully about what I'm doing, particularly turning left at junctions. If there is a lot of traffic, you can just follow someone else. Linda navigates us safely to the Eurocamp site.

After we've unpacked, it's a great relief to be able to just walk. I walk into the town. The sea is a dark blue band, the beach a white strip. There are dozens of villas, many of them still shuttered. Some have embellishments on the rooftops and ridges - figures of cats and manikins. There's a certain air about the houses, something indefinable, almost sinister.

I get a glass of cider in a bar. What does it taste of? I try it tentatively, rolling it around my tongue. And then I realise - apples! French cider tastes of apples, how peculiar. I find a supermarket, buy a couple of bottles of vodka and go back to the campsite.

The moment comes when I'm at the pool on the next day. Me and the kids have practically got it to ourselves. It's hot. The sun slithers crazily all over the surface of the water. The water is cold, but once you get your head under, it's not so bad. This is it; this is France. I've got here all the way from Lancashire. I rest at the side of the pool buoyed by the water. It feels good.

The moment is transient of course. It's quiet because it's a Friday and most people have gone home. Saturday's a different story; when the next week's intake arrive, you can't get near the pool. The weather deteriorates too. It becomes chilly and showery. The English have brought their weather with them, along with their tins of baked beans and cheese slices. And they have to, because although I enjoy visiting the big French supermarkets: Super U and Intermarche, I notice they don't sell English cheese. Now you can go into any Tesco or Sainsburys in England and get all kinds of foreign cheese, French prominent among them, but you'll look in vain for crumbly Lancashire in the dairy section of a French supermarket.

Linda's friends Steve and Karen arrive at the camp site and we have some good days out - to Le Zoo de Cerza, to Bayeux, to Honfleur. We sit out in the evening at their tent, or ours and have long, disorganised meals, with much rushing backwards and forwards for cutlery and plates.

Steve and Karen know their way around and we can usually relax and follow them, but we lose them once in Caen in the tea-time rush-hour. I'm driving panic-struck round huge roundabouts, with not a clue where to go. Caen posed problems for the allies in the last war too. Fortunately Linda keeps her head and navigates us out of trouble.

I've begun to stop worrying about the car, thinking it's going to be OK, and then suddenly it isn't. Driving along in Steve and Karen's wake, I'm aware something's wrong: there's a smell, unaccustomed noise from the engine, and the needle on the temperature gauge is way over in the red. I pull up, tentatively open the bonnet and steam hisses around me. The radiator's empty. I have a bottle of water in the boot and when it's cooled down, I pour it in and we manage to limp back to the camp-site.

Later I discover a split in one of the hoses and manage to bind it up. I spend the rest of the holiday watching the temperature gauge, but the car, satisfied that it's not being taken for granted, behaves itself.

Echoes of war still reverberate. It's why people still visit the area. There are commercial reasons for the museums and monuments, and reconstructions of events. One such is the Son et Lumiere recreating the landing at Pegasus Bridge, which we attend in a downpour, shivering on a bench and feeling uncomfortable for feeling uncomfortable, knowing what it must have been like for the men who were there in June 1944

But would the echoes of war be there anyway, without all the monuments and museums? Would the landscape still be haunted? We go to Arromanches and Ouistreham and visit the beaches: Gold, Juno, Sword. They are quiet now, but is it a stunned stillness following battle?

Uncle Stanley was here, when the sea and beaches were black with men, and the air black with noise. The family tradition is that his wife Mary had waved him off from Portsmouth in the morning and was visiting him in hospital in Southampton in the evening. Whatever the truth of the matter, he survived.

Moving Experiences

Darwen floods its West Pennine valley - a reservoir of stone and brick. The stone predominates, and, as one of its last gestures, Darwen Council offered owners the opportunity to have their homes sandblasted for £5. Most accepted, but here and there you can see one, still stubbornly soot-blackened; the owner too tight-fisted to part with a fiver.

Some of the better housing is on the steeper, western slope. Harwood Street had a toe hold there, running parallel to the valley floor. Our new house was in the row between Crewdson Street and Britten Street. It was a climb to reach it and there was a fair view from the back windows. It was homely within, cosy - curtains, carpets and furnishings displaying bold, bright, indiscriminate colours. The floors were a little uneven. Walls and corners were not quite true. The doors didn't quite shut. Not all the layers of wallpaper, not all the coats of paint could mask this, in fact they exaggerated the homespun, lop-sided effect.

The former owners were a retired couple, an ex-miner and his wife from Barnsley, who had moved there to be nearer the Lancashire coast, but didn't like it, felt they were not accepted by the locals, and were going back home. Prices were already climbing and it cost us £2,000. We got a mortgage from the Council.

On the night we moved in I got five bottles of Lion Crystal from the off-licence at the top of Crewdson Street and drank them watching TV. There was another off-licence at the bottom of Crewdson Street, with a chip shop opposite. The nearest pub was the 'Alex,' just round the corner from there. St George's Church still stood at the end of Harwood Street, but it was derelict and soon to be demolished. There were bonfires on the site before new houses were built.

Our house had a cellar and a steep back yard with a shed underneath, which we ignored. Maybe that gave rise to the dream, I've often had, that I've just discovered some rooms in the house I'd completely forgotten about, neglected rooms with crumbling plaster, but great potential. Once I explored these rooms in my dream, and found a door that led out to a narrow cobbled street, with old, bow-windowed shops, like the street in York Museum.

I don't have fond memories of Harwood Street, maybe because I moved there reluctantly from Billinge Side, maybe because the years I lived there were full of difficulties. My next move had my hallmark characteristics of impulse and haste. When Penny and I divorced I put the house up for sale. The housing market had come to a standstill and nothing happened. The estate agent suggested that I didn't bother with a 'For Sale' sign, there being that many in every street, so I soon forgot that it was for sale. Over a year later a young couple came to view, liked it and wanted to move in straight away.

House prices had continued to rise, even so I wanted a move that had some point to it, a move to a nicer area, to a more interesting house. I looked at an end terraced in Belthorn, which had wonderful views of the moors and the Tower, but it was £9,000. I considered the cottages along the main road in Abbey Village, but these too were beyond me. And then I saw the flats in Sunnyhurst Lane.

The building had been one of the many Co-op shops that had served the suburbs, but had closed back in the 1960s and been converted into two flats. I looked at them both. The downstairs one did not impress me, then we went aloft up the steps at the side. Here was a huge lounge with a split-level ceiling. Three tall windows gave a view of the moors, over the roofs of the houses opposite. There were three bedrooms, a kitchen and bathroom. All the rooms were just separated by wood partitions. Originally upstairs would have been the store room - a big, open space.

There was something about it, maybe I was just recognising my destiny, but I said I'd have it. Buying flats wasn't much done then, and I paid too much - £7,000, but I felt under pressure to move and as it was had to stay with friends, Dave and Gerry, for a few weeks before the flat sale went through.

I liked the flat, liked the area, but never felt I had roots there. I went to the Sunnyhurst Hotel a few times, with a view to becoming a regular, and I made a point of standing at the bar and getting into conversation, but my newsagent was a regular too, and I had a habit of forgetting to pay his bills, so he was cool. Also I didn't quite know who I was, didn't know if I should pretend to share the views and interests of the others; offering shrewd judgements on Rovers' latest signing, getting indignant about taxes etc, or whether I should try and find a true and consistent line for myself. I gave up and stayed in at night with a bottle of Strongbow.

It was a cold flat. The central heating didn't make much impact on such a big room and the gas fire was feeble. I tried to replace it, but lost it altogether, when the fitter discovered there was no proper flue. The ceiling over the third bedroom leaked. I used to have dreams about rain coming in everywhere, still do. The first roofer was a cowboy. He came back a few times, but to no avail, the next time it rained I would soon hear the drip, drip into the bucket. I got somebody in the end, who did the job properly, replacing the lead.

I went for walks in the woods, and up to the Tower, and beyond. I got to know Stanley Bradley, the taxidermist, who lived on nearby Prospect Ave. He used to dress in a kilt and play the pipes outside his house. He knew the moors well; his father had been a gamekeeper. I was semi-comfortable there, like someone in a luke-warm bath, who knows it will be colder when he gets out. Eventually though it gets colder even if you stay put, and 1983 came, the year when things had to change. Moving house had not been part of the plan, but I met Fiona. We married and children came along.

Like the cottage at Billinge, the flat wasn't ideal for children. There were a lot of steps to get up, not easy with a pram or pushchair, so we put the flat up for sale. It was difficult to gauge its worth; there were few flats about. I put 'For Sale' notices in the window, intending to ask £15,000, but there were no takers. It went via an estate agent for £12,500 in the end.

There were not many houses for sale at the time. We looked at one at the other end of Darwen, in Cyprus Street, where oddly enough I'd been to a party many years ago. We bought it, the price was £15,000. Internally it was similar to Harwood Street, the same lop-sidedness and overdone décor. The location though was leafier and more refined.   Opposite was Ashleigh Barrow, where William Shorrock Ashton, cotton manufacturer, had built a villa. When its foundations were being dug, Romano-British burial urns had been found. Oddly the area had long been shunned at night by folk afraid of boggarts. It was as though some kind of racial memory of it being a burial ground had survived.

The villa had been demolished not long before we arrived. The grounds remained with their great chestnut trees. Ashleigh had been divided into flats, and later used by the County Council for evening classes. There was some deliberation about what to do with the site. Should it be used for garages? Should new houses be built? Should it be a playground? In the end picnic tables were put there and a reconstruction of the barrow was created. The gates were removed. It became a good place for children to play. William and Emily played there. Of course at night it was attractive to older children, experimenting with alcohol, glue and solvents.

There were quite a few shops on Bolton Road then - greengrocers, butchers, pet shop, chip shop, grocers. Ashleigh School had a good name, William and Emily were happy there. The neighbours, June and Mrs Ellison on one side, and Tom and Joan on the other were very pleasant. Whitehall Park was not far away; the moors not much further. It seemed we'd be there a long time. There were old folk's homes all around and the cemetery just up the road. It seemed to me that the only way I'd leave there would be in a box, but I was wrong. I was there a long time; seventeen years, but the unexpected happened and I found myself contemplating a move westward to Leyland.

Christmas at Ravenglas

To see it now, enthroned on the hearth with its massive surround, you'd think it had always been there, that the Great Barn at Higher Ghylls Farm had been built around it. Just as the altar dominates the nave of a church, so this monolithic, cast-iron stove commands the space around it. And yet it was installed within living memory, brought overland from the Cumbrian coast on a December day of pewter skies and sleet.

Wood-burning stoves are altars, altars for the worship of fire, and when they are in full spate, what images glow within. Worshippers sit enraptured, viewing dramas of creation and destruction. I've had the care of a few stoves over the years - some have become roaring furnaces at the touch of a match; some have smouldered malevolently; some have belched smoke and flame back into the room like souls possessed by demons.

Nearly ninety per cent of the heat from an open fire goes up the chimney; only one out of every ten bags of coal you buy warms the room. With wood-burning stoves the heat loss is only a third of that. When they're burning well, ticking as the metal expands, they transform the room, nay the house. The heat hits you as you come down the stairs. How anybody can prefer radiators and gas-fires is beyond me. It's as though someone could prefer a china cat on the hearth to a real one. Of course some would - a real cat spits, a real cat scratches, a real cat makes a mess, a real cat needs feeding.

I first saw Higher Ghylls when I was nineteen, though I didn't see it that first time; it was too dark. It was night. Ringo, who lived there, had been a friend of Barney's, who shared a flat with me in Leeds. I'd got to know him when Barney invited him down to our parties. He invited me up to see the farm. I travelled by train to Long Preston and waited in the Maypole Inn. This was in the 1960s when you could upset people by having long hair, indeed Ringo was so called because of his long hair, and had been expelled from Settle School because of it.

I was used to being refused service in pubs and thought, in such an out-of-the-way place, I'd more chance of being lynched than served. In the event there was no problem and the one or two drinking quietly there observed me affably enough. If I'd had more confidence I could have chatted, but I took my beer to a corner and waited.

Ringo arrived at last with his father, Maurice, a farmer with a weathered face and iron grey hair sprouting from under his flat cap. He appraised me good-humouredly, had a glass of beer, exchanged greetings with those at the bar, and then we were out and climbing into an ancient Land Rover for a ride through the darkness.

There were no lights, no moon, no stars. I could see only what the headlights picked up: the ditch and the dry-stone walls on either side of the lane. After several miles of this, we turned off and plunged down a track, the old Land Rover pitching like a small boat in a squall. We came to rest in the farm yard. Dogs barked and rattled their chains.

In the kitchen there was light, and warmth from a huge Aga. Ringo's mother, May, rose to greet me with the gentility and graciousness of a bygone age. It made me think somehow that this was how a guest might have been greeted at Haworth parsonage in the time of the Bronte's. I knew I was welcome at Higher Ghylls.

I became a regular visitor. For a long time it still seemed a remote and inaccessible place. When I was living in Blackburn, I caught the Clitheroe bus to Slaidburn and walked. One night when I was alone on the road, a car came towards me, turned round and pulled up. 'Do you want a lift?' a young woman enquired. In some alarm I assured her I had only a little way to go. 'Get in you fool,' a voice growled. It was Ringo. 'It's only my sister.'

Later I got a motorbike, and later still a car, and then it didn't seem quite so much like going to the ends of the Earth.

It had long been Ringo's plan to do up the barn, to put a bar in. It had been full of cows the first time I'd seen it, but they were long gone. The roof needed doing, and the floor in the hayloft. I'd fallen through once. Fortunately there was enough good wood to arrest me, and I only fell about two feet, but it was a jolt and made me think what the ultimate drop must have been like, the one when you had a rope round your neck.

When the 'Dog and Partridge' at Tosside closed, Ringo got some of the fixtures and fittings. The pub's last day coincided with the London Marathon and he drove down to compete in that, drove back to be in time for last orders, and walked home with the bar. Later he acquired the pool table, stools, optics and a brass foot-rail. He put a toilet in the Barn, and beds up in the hayloft.

All he needed was a stove to warm the place - a big one. He got to know of one for sale in a holiday cottage on the Cumbrian coast near Ravenglass, and arranged to stay the night there and collect it. He borrowed a sturdy trailer, took his son Nathan along to help and invited me. It was a couple of weeks before Christmas. It was a long drive in the shadow of Lakeland's southern fells, past Coniston and Black Combe to the remote and neglected Cumbrian coast. Ravenglass was deserted. It was growing dark by the time we located the cottage.

The old stove had been disconnected and stood in a corner, a black and brooding mass. There was a new stove in the hearth space, a smaller one, a more modern one. We soon had this one all aglow. It made the old one look even blacker and more forbidding. Ringo tested the weight of it, trying to lift it at one corner. It didn't budge, not a millimetre. It might have been fused to the Cumbrian rock with roots of cast iron. We decided to tackle it in the morning.

We had a look outside, picked our way over the waste at the back of the cottage. It was too dark to go far. A rope rapped against a pole in the wind, making a mournful wail, like that of a soul lost on the marshes. Out there somewhere was the sea, the Cumbrian sea which out-broods the brooding fells. Further up the coast were the artificial lights of Sellafield. We drove there later, past estates of glum housing and got fish and chips from a van parked on a vast car-park.

The moment struck when we'd driven back and left the car to go to the pub. The only light came from the windows of the cottages. It was wet underfoot and there was dampness in the air, not rain, not quite rain. There was nobody stirring, not a car passed us. There was no sound. There was only the lights from the cottages. Some of the windows displayed Christmas trees, trees that bore coloured lights like illuminated berries. Behind them the rooms were in darkness. The glow of the lights was reflected in the double-glazing and hazily sketched on the damp street.

This was the moment. This glimpse of other people's Christmases, glamorous, unattainable Christmases, Christmases that were perhaps beyond the comprehension of outsiders such as we were. We were just granted a glimpse, a brief moment of illumination.

We were outsiders in the pub too. It was quite full and we were literally on the edge of things, drinking standing up near the doors. The only attention we attracted was when we went to the bar, and that only tardily and reluctantly granted.

The next day we tackled the brooding, cast-iron mass. We got the trailer up against the back door and stripped the stove of any fittings that could be removed. Nathan was barely fifteen, but was already heavily built and powerful. Ringo had the strength too, but more importantly, strength seasoned with experience. I had neither, so fluttered ineffectually on the periphery, exhorting and wincing, as they coaxed and walked the stripped-down stove to the back door. It was no easy matter threading it through the doorway and over the threshold into the trailer, but the job was done and much relieved, I wiped the sweat from my brow.

The trailer was manhandled round to the front, hitched up to the car and we were off. We took it very steadily going back along the coast and through the Cumbrian hills.

The stove was enthroned at last in its new setting. Many's the night since I've watched it roaring away, outdoing the merriest company in good cheer and warmth. It has become the heart, and maybe the soul, of the Great Barn at Higher Ghylls.

North

In the end you just want to get there. However much you try to persuade yourself that the journey is part of the holiday, in the end you just want the road to stop unravelling before your tired eyes. You just want to get there. This is especially true when your destination is the far north, the far north coast of Scotland, a destination five hundred miles away, but that came much later. My first trip to Scotland was by motorbike in 1983.

That was the year when I'd decided I had to do more. I'd looked at the map of Scotland. The tip of a peninsula, the Mull of Galloway, had drawn my eye and I decided to go. I strapped my camping gear on to the back of my Suzuki X7 and set off after work. I stopped overnight at the camp-site near Castlerigg at Keswick. In the next tent was a chap with his young family. We got talking and he confessed he envied me, envied me my freedom to pack my bags and set off. I had a glimpse of myself as a heroic figure, a man with no name, a high plains drifter, but secretly I felt a bit of a fraud, secretly I felt lonely and nervous.

You cross the border into Scotland and head for Dumfries. Beyond are long sweeping stretches, where the road parallels the coast-line. The glittering prospects of Wigtown Bay and Luce Bay are dangerously distracting. I rode my bike till I ran out of land, admired the view from Scotland's most southerly point, and then turned back to find a campsite.

Tent up, beans eaten, washing up done and it was still barely five. There's not much to do in a tent, nowhere comfortable to sit. There was a pub, a modern brick pub, with one of those huge, open-plan bar spaces, where a sprinkling of elderly Scots couples were watching a huge TV. It was showing an interminable programme about the royal family. The couples watched in silent deference. I had a few pints. Sometimes a few drinks can turn the dullest programme into something watchable, but not in this case. I gave up.

I went back to my tent and turned in. It was still daylight. It was noisy. Even after dark it was noisy, noisier in fact. The pub had suddenly reinvented itself as a venue for an enthusiastic Scots celebration of music and dance, with pipes and shrill yips and yells, as the company thundered through Scottish reels. It was almost light again by the time I slept.

Years later I went to Hawick. Ringo had given up farming, though not the farm, and was working on the secure unit at Calderstones Hospital near Whalley. A colleague had a flat in Hawick and let it out. It was on the second floor of a solidly built tenement, opposite the Safeways supermarket. It was fussily, floridly, but lovingly furnished with a lot of personal stuff, photos and mementos, and that made us feel more like locals when we went out at night. There were four of us: me and Ringo, Gordon, also from Calderstones and Les, who'd been a colleague of Ringo's years before at Castleberg in Settle, but who now worked in the community in Wigan.

Hawick seems quiet when you go out at 8.00, a couple of hours later though and it's buzzing. Its High Street pubs cater for everybody. I preferred the ones with no music, no TV screen and not many customers, but Les and Gordon wanted a bit more life, a lot more life in Les's case - live music, and that was on offer too.

The police were in evidence, but there was no sense of menace. Everybody seemed friendly, even when some lads enquired about our football allegiances and we admitted to tepid support for Blackburn Rovers, there was no unpleasantness. Of course Blackburn had a long tradition of importing Scots as players and managers. In fact with Fergie Suter back in the 1870s, they probably had the first professional player, though paying players was illegal then. More recently of course, they'd had Kenny Dalgleish and Grahame Souness as managers,

On the morning after it was over the road to Safeways for the 'big breakfast:' fried eggs, bacon, sausages, black puddings, tomatoes, mushrooms, hash browns, fried bread and toast. Everybody seemed to relish it, but in my case it was bravado, and each swallowed mouthful was carefully calculated.

Every souvenir shop between Gretna Green and John O'Groats sells them - postcards being comical at the expense of Scottish weather. There's the 'four seasons' one: four cartoons of glum sheep huddled against the rain, the only things that's different being the caption: spring, summer, autumn, winter.

And that's how it is, especially in the west. If it isn't raining yet, it soon will be. But once it wasn't.

We were in Kintyre at the caravan site at Point Sands, me and my sister Linda and the kids. It had been a long journey, made worse by going through the centre of Glasgow, instead of staying on the M8 and crossing the Firth of Forth over the Erskine Bridge, but the slow moving Saturday afternoon traffic gave us plenty of time to study the city's architecture.

Inveraray always seems like the gateway to the Isles and Highlands, but there's a long winding way by the shores of Loch Fyne before you get to Tarbert and the entrance to Kintyre. It was good to arrive. While Linda unpacked and made the beds, and the kids squabbled about who was sleeping where, I sat on the caravan steps with a cup of tea. It was warm and sunny. I looked up at the sky for the grey clouds. There were none. The sky was serene and blue. It was Spring Bank Holiday week, the end of May and the beginning of June. It was fine the next day and the day after that. It was fine all week. I spent a lot of time sitting on the caravan steps in the sun that week, from the early morning coffee, to the last vodka at eleven at night when it was still light. It was a week of hot blue skies and hot white sand. I've been to Scotland every year since and never had a week like it.

We went to Point Sands a few times, and then one year went further north still to Arisaig. And when we arrived there at our cottage, Miller's Cottage, there came that moment that was the distillation of all such moments of arrival.

The last leg of these forays into Scotland is often the trickiest. You're tired, your patience is running on reserve. It may be growing dark. The directions may be ambiguous. Fortunately Linda's navigation skills got us on the right track, a single one, but it was dusk and there was nothing else on the road.

The big, white, farm-type gate of Millburn Cottage stood open. I turned in and parked on the grass next to a four wheel drive vehicle. The cottage door stood open and the owner an Englishman, came out to greet us. He did his spiel in the style of a jolly school master. I let Linda deal with him and had a look round.

We stood near the head of the sea loch, Loch Nan Ceall. The sea was still. Behind the cottage a wooded hill rose steeply to Loch Mhuilinn, which supplied the water for the cottage, brown with peat, as we found later much to Frances's consternation, when she saw her bath-full. There were outbuildings with a generator, logs and a boat.

When the owner had gone. We could appreciate the silence. It was cold enough for a fire. There was a stove in the lounge, a Morso Squirrel, with a squirrel embossed on the side. I soon got it going, sending shadows dancing round the walls. We unpacked.

Linda started dinner. The kids were down at the water's edge. I had a look round the cottage, in all the bedrooms, noseying in cupboards and drawers.

I opened a bottle of wine and took my glass outside. It was light still out on the water, but growing dark in the shadow of the wooded hill. This place was somewhere special.

I went down to join the kids. The tide was flooding imperceptibly, the ripples like flowing glass. Emily was sitting on a large rock. The sea had almost encircled it.

"I've seen seals," she said, "and a sea-otter."

There were tears in her eyes at the wonder of it.

That was the moment.

The 500 mile journey was made years later. There were the kids and their respective boyfriend and girlfriend, me and Sandy. We were bound for Kirtomy near Thurso, about as far north as you can get. Again I'd agreed to it months before on a vodka lit, fire-lit evening, when Emily had picked it out of the brochure as being the only one with the right accommodation and location.

It was the end of October, half-term week. I was both excited and nervous. It was a long way. The Toyota Camry was relaxing and reliable, but there was 150,000 miles on the clock. Would it let us down? William and his girlfriend were already touring Scotland and we were to pick them up at Thurso railway station. We got away not much after 6.00. Emily, her boyfriend, and Sandy fell asleep.

The M6 was quiet and we made steady progress. It was fine, - mild blue skies and incipient sunshine. All the way to Scotland it was fine; all the way to Glasgow it was fine. Then we hit fog, dense, implacable fog. This was bad. This was going to slow us down. Then it got worse: a sign appeared saying the M73 was closed. How could they do it? How could they just close a motorway? I'd planned my route and, as always, had it taped to the dashboard: M6, A74, M74, M73, A80, M80 and A9. Of course I should have gone on-line and checked for traffic problems before we set off. Too late - now what?

My passengers slept on. Maybe Sandy stirred, picking up my agitation. There were diversion signs, but I knew from experience, how they can disappear, or be ambiguously sited, and following them in dense fog...

I did follow them as well as I could, and soon found myself passing landmarks I'd passed ten minutes earlier. I was going round in circles. I decided to get on the M8 for Glasgow, hoping there'd be an exit for the A80 going north. There was, at junction twelve.

It was good to be back on track. The fog persisted but became intermittent around Stirling and then went altogether, and we were bowling along in bright sunshine. The kids woke up then and we stopped for coffee. Sandy got out to have a pee and stretch her legs. An uneventful journey for them.

The A9 goes on for ever. It's the road to the Highlands, built so the English could subdue the clansmen. There are stretches of dual carriageway, but often you're wallowing along in the wake of a labouring truck. We got to Perth and then the long stretch, the long climb to the Cairngorms, Scotland's ski country. We stopped at Pitlochry for the toilets.

At Inverness the Saturday morning traffic slowed us down, and then we crossed the Moray Firth to the Black Isle, and then Cromarty Firth, and then Dornoch Firth, and then the A9 becomes a coastal road all the way to Wick. We turned off for Thurso across a stretch of empty Highlands.

I'd pictured Thurso as a sleepy village clustered round its railway station. It turned out to be a busy town with not a sign I could see pointing to the station. I'd been driving for nearly ten hours. I didn't feel too bad, but I didn't want any problems at this stage. I managed to squeak into a parking space on the Co-op supermarket and we set off on foot. We had to ask a succession of people before we found the station, but fortunately William and girlfriend were waiting there when we located it. We did some shopping at the Co-op and then were away on the last leg.

We followed a quiet road to Scrabster where there were ferries to the Orkneys, passed Dounreay Nuclear Power Station, where later we found signs advising that children and pets should not be allowed on the beach because of high radiation levels, and then turned down a narrow road towards the sea and Kirtomy. The house was just past the phone box: a detached, white building, with chimneys and dormer windows at either end, and a large central porch. I drove up round the side and stopped - such a relief to be able to switch off the engine.

The owner, a retired policeman, was there to greet us. He'd lit a cheerful coal fire. It was a genuine welcome. He showed us the window at the side of the lounge, which looked out to sea, said there'd be Naval manoeuvres during the week and left his field glasses.

I enjoyed the fire and the sense of 'mission accomplished.' The kids sorted out their rooms and decided who was cooking what for tea. Later we took a walk down to the sea before it got dark.

Looking out from the cliffs there was nothing much between us and the North Pole. I'd driven to the very end of 'Terra Firma.' I didn't linger. There was a cold wind blowing and I'd an appointment to keep with an ice-cold vodka by the fire.

Careering On

They called her the 'Ice Queen,' but I always thought there was a great deal of warmth in her pale blue regard. Barbara Snell was Librarian for Ribble Valley and based at Whalley Library. The demands of the library service left her with spare capacity. Rather like the librarians of an earlier age; WA Abram at Blackburn for instance, who was also editor of The Blackburn Times and author of topographical works, Barbara Snell could have done much more.

Her deputy, Sue Holden, was another vivid, capable woman, but her skills were more narrowly focussed. She put all her energies into the day-to-day running of the library service. They were two formidable personalities and didn't always see eye to eye. The pale blue regard of the one met the green gaze of the other, and neither faltered.

This is the situation I came into in 1984. I've never discovered why it took so long to decide to offer me the job. I suspect Barbara and Sue were holding out for their own candidate and Mike Dolan thought they should have a change, but I don't know. A change is what they got however.

I brought a lot of enthusiasm with me. I was full of ideas. Whalley though was pretty well sorted out and there was a general feeling that I was changing things for the sake of it. There was a conflict: I was there, thinking to effect great improvements and innovations, and they just wanted somebody to make sure the petty cash balanced and the cleaners didn't run out of floor polish.

The users too were not fond of re-arrangements. They knew the library well and liked things the way they were. They were a knowledgeable, demanding lot and came in with lists of requests culled from the literary supplements. By way of a complete change there would occasionally be a Calderstones patient buzzing about like a trapped bluebottle. Calderstones was a big mental hospital then, before 'care-in-the-community' slimmed it down. It was just round the corner from the library, up Mitton Road.

I liked it best when I could get out of the library. I had to take books to old folks' homes. Sometimes I worked at Mellor Library, or Read or Clitheroe. Sometimes I went out on the mobiles. There were two; a big one that parked up in the villages, and a small one that would go down tracks to individual farms. The countryside population was dwindling; most people were out during the day. The country was becoming where people wanted to live, or have second homes, and a lot of farms were now desirable residences, whose owners either worked, or lived, in nearby towns. Often Jim, the driver, would inch the van down a narrow track only to find nobody at home.

"Why the heck can't they ring up and say?" he would remark, only more colourfully.

It was on the van that I first went to Harrop Fold. One of the readers invited us into her Elizabethan farmhouse for a cup of tea. With its exposed oak beams, deep, mullioned windows, huge fireplace and inglenooks, it was like a glimpse of heaven. My converted Co-op flat at Sunnyhurst in Darwen didn't seem much cop in comparison.

I wasn't needed at Whalley. The post of Reference Librarian came up at Chorley and I went for that. It was a new post, created in conjunction with the move to new central premises. Historically mid-Lancashire towns like Chorley and Leyland had been reluctant to burden the rates with library services and had been slow to provide facilities. The location of Chorley's old central library was indicative of this; in Gillibrand Street, well away from the centre.

'This can't be right,' I thought to myself as I made my way there on interview-day, 'I'm going away from the town here,' but it was. That modest building, modest in size, modest in appearance, modestly located, was the central library.

I was renewing my acquaintance with Jim Heyes, who was deputy there and had worked at Blackburn. Chief Librarian was Duncan Farquhar, a man who chose his words carefully and left nothing to chance. The preparations for the move were well advanced and Duncan had a firm hold on things. There was little for us to do but follow meticulous instructions. The new central library was as central as you could get, opposite the bus station. It was in the building that had housed the teacher training college. Unfortunately not all the building was devoted to the library, and there was a lack of space from the very beginning. The reference library was handicapped by having no stack, nowhere for back-files, previous editions, nor valuable items.

Jim was at heart a reference and local history man and we had similar ideas about how things should be done. We worked well together. For a while it was interesting, but once everything was sorted out and we were up and running, I got restless again. Incidentally the new reference library featured the Prestel service, a forerunner of PCs. It sat on the enquiry desk, its screen all aglow with expectation, but it was little used. It was quicker to look information up in a directory. Nevertheless it was a harbinger.

Accrington next, and again a new job in a new library. In 1988 the former Mechanics' Institute in Accrington was refurbished to provide accommodation for a local history library and the Registrar's office. I was appointed as the new Local Studies Librarian. Again I was involved with a library on the move, and again I arrived to find a formidable team already in place.

Josie Green was Reference Librarian and a keen local historian, as were Helen Barrett and Catherine Duckworth, who job-shared the Reference Assistant's post, as was Brian Ashton, Chief Librarian and former Reference Librarian. The Assistant Local Studies Librarian was Mike Clarke, *the* authority on canals who, was working on his definitive history of the Leeds Liverpool Canal. In addition there was an enthusiastic local history group which included author Bill Turner, who'd written a definitive history of the Accrington Pals, the celebrated researchers Jack and Catherine Broderick and the indefatigable June Huntingdon, the sort of no-nonsense Lancashire lass who had enough nous and get-up-and-go to turn the world on its head. It was hard to feel I had much to contribute in such company.

Accrington has a strong sense of identity, reinforced by, if not a result of, the fate of the Pals and the fame of its football team, Accrington Stanley. A name that resonates still, though it's many years since it featured in the Saturday teatime results round-up.

I felt most comfortable in the company of the caretaker there, Albert. He was unfailingly good-humoured, always ready to help. Whenever I had a project on the go, making something for the kids, he'd get involved. I made a model pirate ship for William one Christmas, and he scoured the model shops for a pair of brass cannon for it. He'd been widowed a number of years and filled the void by making himself useful to others. It was the kind of attitude you came across frequently in Accrington. I enjoyed my three years there.

Lancaster next. 'Light on Old Lancaster' was the title of a book of old photographs I published when I worked there. And there is something special about the light, perhaps it's the river that adds luminosity. You notice it in the evening. Night arrives stealthily, the sunset glow lingers over the water and on the castle walls. Of course the past is all around you, and perhaps the light from ancient days seeps into the present.

Librarian Steve Eccles invited me up for a chat. I went on the train. It was a sunny day. It was a fairly relaxed, low-key conversation. The sun lay on the desk between us. There seemed no great urgency about anything. I'd applied for the post of Reference Librarian. I didn't know that nobody else had applied. I didn't know that this was an interview. After we'd talked about this and that for a while, he offered me the job.

I felt pleased, waiting for the train back in the sunny station. It seemed like a glorious golden chapter was about to begin. And in some ways, yes it was, and in some ways...

Lancaster Library's the biggest for miles in every direction. It holds sway over Yorkshire and Cumbria as well as Lancashire. My predecessor Ethel Geddes had built up a splendid collection of material on all three counties, and had maintained meticulous records. I could not pretend to pass myself off as a worthy successor, and indeed her mantle sat more naturally on the shoulders of her understudy, my assistant, Susan Wilson.

I reorganised and rationalised, always a good thing to do when you're out of your depths - change everything, create systems only you understand.

On the basis of Morecambe always having been a favourite resort for Yorkshire folk, I transferred the Yorkshire collection there, into the care of the capable and keen Lyn Wilman. I offered duplicated material to Lancaster University. I slimmed the collection down.

Lancaster had been a record repository and there were thousands of manuscripts, many of them in a strong-room under the museum. Only a gaoler from the infamous Chateau D'If would have felt comfortable retrieving anything from down there. I was able to relocate everything and at least the collection was all under one roof, if not all together.

Despite friendships with Karen Davies, Sue Parky and Andrew Otway, I never felt quite at home at Lancaster. I could have fancied that another library altogether existed, one that excluded me - a parallel service, dealing in darker matters. Some of my colleagues served elsewhere, had different allegiances. Although we worked side by side day after day, what they saw was not what I saw, the world they graced was not one that I could enter. We didn't even talk the same language really.

Already a wind was blowing, a wind that would turn into a hurricane, blowing books away, blowing them out of libraries up and down the land. You sometimes think what's happening locally is just that, just something that's happening to you. The evidence before your eyes doesn't always suggest the bigger picture.

Lancaster was short of space. Few libraries were built with future needs in mind, but the situation was acute at Lancaster. The weeding out of books began. Books were being withdrawn, which to me, and other, older, bookish people, seemed indispensable, books that to me should be available at any decent sized library, even if years went by without them being read, or consulted. I was out of date. The idea of the library as a repository of culture and knowledge was being undermined, often by people with little knowledge and less culture - people who made decisions based on the last date stamped in the book. Though of course it wasn't that. It wasn't a decision at all. Evolutionary forces were stirring. It was an information revolution, *the* Information Revolution a revolution that was going to change the world just as much as the Industrial Revolution of the eighteenth and nineteenth centuries had.

Before I left Lancaster, a PC arrived in the reference department. It didn't do anything. It was never switched on. Nobody knew what to do with it, but it was there. Inert, alien, waiting to be activated, waiting for the signal.

Allonby Adventure

There was Gerry and Annemarie from Blackburn Library, Dave, Gerry's husband, and me. We had a cottage booked on the Cumbrian coast. We got away mid-afternoon, but in early December, the darkness soon catches up with you, and it overtook us while we were still on the M6. It was raining. White lights streamed towards us and red lights streamed away.

I was driving. There must be deposits of optimism in my make-up: I always imagine setting off for a few days to be a matter of open roads and sunshine, but on this occasion, as so often, it was filthy weather and traffic queues. The spray from lorries overwhelmed my wipers, blinding me at speeds in excess of 70 mph.

It wasn't much better when we exited at junction 40 for the A66 to Keswick. I find it difficult driving at night when there are no street lights. It doesn't bother most people. They race through the dark at daylight speeds, and overtake with bends looming in their headlights. Maybe they do have radar. I sometimes try to hang on to their tail-lights, but they're too fast. I lose them, and end up with a queue of headlights behind me, shimmering, simmering with impatience. It was harder still this night with the driving rain.

In the blackness ahead were the heights of Blencathra and Threlkeld Common. I bypassed Keswick, where folk were arriving home from work to cheery firesides, and stayed on the A66 through Braithwaite. It was at Braithwaite where I had my first camping holiday, 40 years earlier. It hadn't been a happy experience. I'd been laid low with home-sickness. Occasionally my spirits were lifted by illicit pints of Lakeland beer, but I couldn't cope and went home early, much to the dismay of my companion Brian Mosley. How we cling to the familiar, to habits and habitat, and yet nothing's permanent, nothing lasts. Maybe that's why we do it.

Going through Wythop Wood, we caught black glimpses of Bassenthwaite Lake, and then turned away for Cockermouth and Maryport. The Lake District completely upstages the coast. Where else does that happen? Where else is the sea trumped by greater glories inland? Nowhere, and the Cumbrian coast is in a permanent sulk about it. Maryport even turns its back on the sea, pretending it's not there.

We headed up-coast for Allonby. In the darkness on the left, the sea surged and retreated, in the darkness on the right the lights of lonely farmhouses twinkled amid the black fields. And then we reached the subdued lights of Allonby. The rain was mildly persistant.

Allonby's named after Alan, Second Lord of Allendale, who, it is said, had a melancholy strain and found the view across the Solway Firth to distant Criffel agreeable. Our cottage, 'Roseacre,' was in the corner of the cobbled market square. It was built in 1824 when the population of the village was a little over 700, and William Wordsworth was living not many miles away at Rydal Mount in Ambleside, his reputation as England's foremost poet already established. Fishing for herring was carried on, as was handloom weaving, but most were employed in agriculture.

Allonby was for a time a popular bathing resort and the baths, built in 1835, are still there, as is the 'Ship Hotel,' where Charles Dickens and Wilkie Collins stayed, when they were engaged on their "Two Idle Apprentices" tour.

There was only just enough light, both in the street and in the house, as though any great illumination would have shown too much, given too much away, a hangover perhaps from the smuggling days, when many of the dark houses of Allonby would have had casks of rum and French brandy hidden away. 'Roseacre' had a nautical air, not hard to imagine the ghostly, subterranean rumblings of men with barrels.

Saturday morning was brighter. Dave went out for a look-round and to smoke his pipe. I crossed the empty road to the empty beach and observed the calm respiration of the sea. There was a bright, golden sheen on the Solway Firth that was beaten thinly and stretched all the way to Scotland's caravan coastline, Kippford, where we often used to stay, purple Criffel and rosy Sweetheart Abbey.

Silloth is a short drive away up the coast. A port was created here in the mid-nineteenth century, an outlet for industrious Carlisle. It became a resort too for the city's holiday-makers. Its situation and climate recommended it. Grand hotels and broad avenues graced the open, grassy space of the 'Green'. It's not a noted resort now and there was little Saturday morning bustle to enliven it. We investigated the charity shops.

That first echo of other times struck me, of other worlds, of something strange. On the face of it the good people of Silloth were just going about their Saturday morning business, shopping, enjoying that relaxed, weekend feeling; no rush to get kids to school, or get to work, but it just wasn't quite convincing. Were we being stealthily observed? Was a show of normality being put on for our benefit?

We banished such fanciful notions by driving inland and visiting Cockermouth, a market town of reassuring normality, unfeignedly absorbed in commercial activity, attracting tourists, selling the

Lake District and its Wordsworth connections. Wordsworth's house was closed for restoration to its eighteenth century condition. It was built in 1745. Sir James Lowther bought it in 1761 and John Wordsworth, William's father, who was Sir James' agent, moved in in 1766. Wordsworth was born there on the 7th of April 1770. When his mother died in 1778 Wordsworth moved away to be cared for by relatives. In 1937 the house was threatened with demolition to make way for a bus station, but survived to become a National Trust property.

As December darkness threatened, we returned to the coast. I remembered long-ago, December tea-times, with hot, buttered crumpets by the fire, the teapot on the hearth, football scores, and Dixon of Dock Green on the television, with Christmas twinkling on the horizon.

The fields were fading fast, as we ran into the shadows of Maryport. The Romans had been here and built a fort, later the area was part of Scotland. Humphrey Senhouse made the port and named it after his wife.

We found somewhere to park near the harbour. The wind had got up and was well peppered with rain. The tethered boats jostled restlessly. The streets were ill-lit, as though the power were failing. Shops were on the point of closing. We bought bread in a 1950s style corner shop and were served by a lean, dark woman with quick, bright eyes. I saw her sister a moment later in the street, as we took shelter from a sudden squall under a flapping awning. She darted us a quick, curious glance as she flitted by.

There was little traffic in the streets, no people at all in such inclement weather - yes, one there was, one who stood on the corner and watched us, another sister of the shopkeeper, or a near relative. We hurried, heads bowed, back to the car. It was then that the notion struck me that we were on the very edge of discovering the secret of Maryport, of seeing beyond the veil, beyond the shadows.

I was half glad to be in the company of the others and half frustrated. It struck me that together we were too many to deal with, to assimilate, but had I been alone... If I'd been alone, then one of the sisters, one of the haggard, Celtic beauties would have crooked her gnarled finger and I would have followed.

We gained the safety of the car and drove up the dark, coast road back to Allonby. A former colleague of Dave's from Blackburn College, Andy, who was teaching in Carlisle, joined us for the evening, and we repaired to the Ship Hotel for an excellent dinner.

On the next morning the sun shone with unabashed brilliance, as though to banish all the silly notions of the night before. The four of us walked along the beach. I searched the shingle for treasure, for washed-up doubloons, or Roman gold. I wandered, apart from the others, went down towards the sea, to the flat, hard sand that still gleamed from the receding tide.

What were those marks that curved gracefully away? Footprints - the prints of a woman's bare feet! They ran all the way to the sea, where they were lost in the waves. In all the long expanse of empty beach, in either direction, there were none returning.

Hollands Cottage

As I've said I never thought I would leave. I thought I could see my future. When I was too old to live alone, there would be the nursing home, then the grave in Darwen Cemetery. I never thought I would be able to sell the house, thought that my neglect of it had put it beyond the pale, that if it remained standing for as long as I did, then that was the best that could be hoped for.

And then of course there was the gross inflation of house prices. What could I possibly afford that would be any better, or even as good? Darwen had been a black hole as far as housing went. It was cheap, so people were attracted, but because it was cheap you could never get out again, never escape.

Of course there was always renting, and I looked sometimes at what there was, but the insecurity of it scared me. I couldn't do it. I would stay in Cyprus Street to the bitter end. It wasn't so bad, quite cosy at night with the wood-burning stove ticking away and the vodka flowing, ice cold from the fridge. That would do for me. I didn't take into account though how circumstances combine. Big changes can result when a number of small changes come together. Like road accidents; most drivers can cope with one unexpected occurrence, but when there are a few together: bad weather conditions, a car awkwardly parked; someone going too fast, a lapse of concentration...

I think I've made it clear how I envied people who had interesting houses. On walks in the Dales and bike rides through the Ribble Valley, I would see these wonderful houses and feel bitter that I would never be able to live anywhere like that. What had those who lived in such places done to be so blessed? Were they somehow harder-working, more talented, more determined than me? Probably, but in some cases I suppose they were just lucky. Would you feel lucky? Would it be a permanent blessing to have such a home, to have beamed ceilings and inglenooks and window-seats and half-landings and studies and libraries and billiard rooms and several bathrooms and fourth and fifth bedrooms and french windows and utility rooms and wine cellars and walled gardens and kitchen gardens and outbuildings and garages and driveways? Or do you end up taking all that for granted? Does the house, however grand, become just where you live?

I still built castles in the air, or rather substantial stone dwellings on quiet coastal roads, with sea views and footpaths down to the beach, and vaulted cellars, whence smugglers tunnels led to caves, but I didn't expect to live in one, nor do I still, but I didn't expect to leave Cyprus St and it happened.

Circumstances were compelling me to consider a move to Leyland. I needed to be near Runshaw College for William and Emily's benefit. I didn't know what my house was worth. We'd paid £15,000 many years before, had tried to sell it for £30,000 at one point without success, but it was 2003 and people were talking £50,000 and more for such houses. Whatever, I knew I couldn't afford anything worth having in Leyland. Was renting a sensible option? Everybody said no - dead money, no security, never get back on the property ladder etc.

The more you think about things, the more reasonable they seem. I started looking at 'to-let' ads in the property pages, and driving out to see what some of them looked like. It was by chance though that I saw the big house on Southport Road at the junction with Leyland Lane, just next to the car showrooms and garage on the corner. The 'to-let' sign was a homespun thing and it made me think that here might be a bargain, here might be the place that was meant to be. I rang the number and it was no bargain at £650 a month, but I arranged to view. It was big - four bedrooms - just, the fourth was a box-room. The kitchen was vast like a hotel kitchen. There were two reception rooms, there was a bend in the stair which added a gracious touch, but there was something a bit cold about it and the garage at the back was a bit too close for comfort. You could hear the men at work - the bangings and the banter. I wasn't sure, and really, to take such a step, you do have to be sure.

I thought about it and came back again and again to look at it. In the end I decided, yes, and rang up - it had gone.

I went back to the property pages and found the ideal place: Hollands Cottage, next to Leyland Golf Club, within easy walking distance of Runshaw, big garden, wood-burning stove. I rang - it had gone. I saw another I liked on Longmeaneygate, a bit dear at £700, but secluded and near major routes. I rang - it had gone. I wandered further afield and saw somewhere at Walmer Bridge, a corner property with a big garden and french windows. I made an appointment to view and began to envisage living there. The day before my appointment I got a phone call to say someone had taken it.

The fact was there wasn't much rented property and anything good went at once. It was beginning to seem impossible. I drove past Hollands Cottage now and again and the 'to-let' sign was still there, even weeks after my enquiry. I rang the estate agent. It had come back on the market. I asked for an appointment to view but was told it would have to be at the end of the week; other people were looking.

I went back. The garden was enormous - like a field. The Golf Club rather overlooked the property. I wondered if there would be noise at night, with people coming and going. I peered through the windows as best I could. The kitchen looked OK. The room described as the dining room didn't look big enough for a dolls' tea party. What should I do? Chances were whoever saw it before me would take it. I made a rash decision, went to the estate agent and said I'd have it without seeing it.

What had I done? Not only put my security at risk, but that of the kids too. The landlord was the Worden Estate. They owned many properties in Leyland, as well as the Golf Club. Suppose they decided to knock Hollands Cottage down to expand the Golf Club car-park; suppose they decided to double the rent; suppose a sprig of the Worden dynasty wanted a little place; supposing I lost my job. My mortgage at Cyprus Street was so small I could have managed it, even out-of-work. There would have been a roof over our heads until the end of my days, and it would have been there for the kids after I'd gone. Hollands Cottage was £600 a month, more than I could afford without subsidising it with money from selling Cyprus St. Moving house is a stressful enough life-event, and I'd compounded it by adding insecurity and financial worries. And yet there was the garden...

It was July when we moved in and the evening primrose glowed at night like lanterns of pale gold. Swifts and martins made long swooping passes, and, when the sun's demise reddened the sky, the bats made erratic figures around the old, red-brick walls. It was the garden that made the house special. It had been a smallholding once with dozens of hen-huts. Goats had been kept and the remains of the machinery for milking them was still in the outbuildings. The tenants then had turned out into Wigan Road in a pony and trap. Wigan Road was a drawback, constantly busy, often being dug up, with temporary traffic lights in place. We had a cat, Curt, when we first moved. It was only a couple of weeks before it was killed on the road. The cars travel too fast for the youngest and nimblest cats.

In 1745 Bonnie Prince Charles came past our front door with his Highlanders on his way to Derby. Of course Hollands Cottage wasn't there then. Wigan Road was just a rough road through a wilderness, as rough a road as you'd find anywhere in Lancashire, until the Turnpike Trust improved it in the mid 1820s, and installed the mile-stone which still stands outside. Hollands Cottage owes its existence to Henry Holland who had a brick and tile works that stood on the Golf Club site.

For the first time I began to measure the passing of the seasons by nature, rather than by the calendar. In winter there's nothing - merely stark outlines and sullen weeds, and then there are snowdrops. I planted a few the first year, not knowing there were minefields of them already there, waiting to explode, not knowing that they would lie under the hedges and at the edges of the grass like snow, sheltered from the sun. My own efforts straggled here and there in twos and threes.

Daffodils emerge next - cautious, green probes, alien in a landscape of heavy black soil and listless grass. If they grow tall too soon, the retreating winter winds will carry out reprisals. The first ones I planted were sparse and soon brow-beaten, but I've planted a hundred or so bulbs every year since and they're beginning to make a better show.

And, as the days lengthen, the colours deepen: bluebells and forget-me-nots bring lights of contrasting blue to the gloom. The lilac glows. The laburnum lights up. In May all is splashed with blossom; apple and hawthorn, and the pewter limbs of the walnut tree are misted with green. Then the red, incendiary poppies go off. Too heady for their own good; they droop groggily and then lie supine on the grass. And how the grass grows. Fortunately the rent included the cost of someone coming every two weeks to cut it.

I planted peas. The rabbits were grateful and ate all but the last millimetre of stalk. The potatoes did better, as did the onions and cabbage. The cauliflower didn't grow. Veg are cheap enough to buy, too cheap probably, but you grow them to witness the miracle; how the tiny seed becomes the huge cabbage. And you do it for the freshness. The potatoes, in particular, cooked in minutes and tasted better than anything you could buy in the shops.

So it was the garden that soothed me, reassured me when I worried and wondered how long we could afford to live here. The future did not stretch away into a secure old age, and the satisfaction of knowing that the house would pass to descendants. All there was was here and now. And maybe that's the way it should be. Maybe that's the only way to really appreciate things, knowing it's fleeting. Death is a merciless landlord - you can pay off your mortgage and wave your deeds in his face, but he'll still evict you.

I got a Christmas tree from Ringo the first year, and planted it outside the front door. It was touch and go whether it would survive until Christmas, but it did. I put lights on and it twinkled prettily at night, a welcome sight when you turned the corner of the house.

On our first New Year's Eve, I looked out before going to bed. A blizzard was blowing, the snow flying horizontally. The little tree was tossed this way and that like the mast of a vessel in a storm; the lights swinging wildly, a flurry of colour against a backdrop of shimmering white.

It was a moment to remember, one to contrast with the many moments on summer evenings when the shadows gathered round the house and the sky opened up to show you the stars.

White Van Man

And so the dreams of piloting the wine-dark seas and island hopping in the Aegean came down to the van. I'd considered buying a canal boat. Mike Clarke, the Leeds/Liverpool canal man had advised against it, and I felt maybe I wasn't enough of a boat enthusiast to make it work. Also moorings were hard to come by and expensive.

The van was a 1990 Volkwagen Transporter and had been tucked away and used as storage space in Jim's garage for the last five years. It needed a new gearbox and a new exhaust, and some tidying up and re-spraying, before I could take it away and start fitting it out as a camper. It was August 2005. It had been a good summer, not as good as 2003, but better than average. Would there be time to get the van ready for a trip before the weather deteriorated, before it started to get dark at teatime? Would we be able to catch the tail-end of summer?

By now Jim was semi-retired. His son Heath was doing most of the work, but Heath was away with his family in his own van in France. He wouldn't be back till the middle of the month. Jim promised to do as much as he could.

My first thought had been to put the camper van idea back until retirement, get something then with my lump-sum, but wasn't that against all my current thinking? How did I know what my circumstances would be then, or even if I'd still be around? Hadn't the experience of living at Hollands Cottage taught me that all there is is now?

I looked at the campers at Todds, the motor-home dealers at Lostock Hall. For £15,000 you could get something small, but well equipped. I didn't have a tenth of that to spend. Besides, although these vans had everything: cooker, sink, toilet, fridge, shower; they were claustrophobic. They looked OK with nobody in them, but there was barely enough room to move about. What would it be like with three of us and all the baggage? Where would Gordon's packed lunch go?

All I needed was somewhere to sleep, somewhere pleasant to sit in the evening. I needed lighting, and a camping gas cooker to brew up, or warm up a tin of beans. We'd be staying mostly on sites and most campsites have toilets and showers and washing-up facilities.

The original gear box had been four-speed, the replacement was five-speed. This might improve fuel economy and reduce engine noise, but the selection diagram on the gear stick knob now meant nothing. Jim and Heath got on well with it and the van was ready before the end of August. There was a bit of difficulty over insurance; Swinton's didn't do big vans, so I had to find somebody else. Jim drove the van over, so I could start work.

Gordon had had a caravan which we'd all gone away in in 1994 to Bamburgh in Northumberland. That had been its last trip. It had crawled later up to Higher Ghylls to die. Some of its fittings came in handy for the van.

The garden was neglected. I was too busy sawing up plywood

and experimenting with ways of fitting wooden panels to the van. Ideas came and went. I had a brain wave: three functions in one. I made a box which served as storage space, table and support for a bed. I bought a second hand roof rack. I bought loft insulation to go behind the wood panels. I was going to put carpet down, but thinking what the weather's usually like, decided on lino tiles.

The insurance got sorted out. I taxed it for a year and prepared to drive out on to the A49. I tried to remember what Jim had said about the gears - over to the left, push down and pull back for first. I turned too tightly and scraped against the hedge. Anyway I was out into the road. Let the gear stick slip back into the middle and push forward for second. Pull back with a little wiggle for third. Don't bother about fourth now - traffic lights approaching. Stop. The break pedal seemed a long way off the floor. Back into first - over to the left, push down, pull back. Was that first? Was it engaged properly? Releasing the clutch, I only just teetered forward. No, try again. Jim said not to use force, just guide it with your finger tips. Not so easy to remember with an impatient queue behind you, and the lights changing to red again.

The gears take some getting used to. I can't decide if they're awkward, or I am. Two other things: visibility. I'd got used to looking over my shoulders to see what's going on. More than once that glance has saved me from an accident. You can't do this in the van, not to the left anyway. You have to use your mirrors and mirrors are deceitful. Manoeuvring's the other difficulty. This is to do with visibility, but also the steering geometry. You're sitting over the front wheels, so it turns quickly, hence the contact with the hedge.

We're well into September now and trying to arrange for Ringo, Gordon and me all to be off work at the same time isn't easy. It's October before we manage it. Ringo had a friend Liz , who had recently moved to Port William in Dumfries and Galloway. He had a long-standing invitation to visit. We decided to make Port William our inaugural destination and use it as a base for further trips.

This was a perfectly sensible idea for a trip, but I suppose I'd had a more romantic, 'chasing summer' notion – a journey to remote western isles. First of all though I had to use the van to take William and Emily and all their stuff to halls of residence in Manchester, and on the following day, use it as a mobile bookshop to try and sell a few copies of my latest book, 'The Man With No Bike Clips' at a cycle event in Avenham Park in Preston. We'd be setting off for Scotland on the day after that.

I was worried about driving into Manchester on a Saturday morning. We'd had a letter from the university warning that registration and picking up keys was a lengthy business, and begging us to be patient. In the event there was no problem, no waiting. It was soon all sorted, and in a couple of hours I was finding my way out of Manchester alone in an empty van.

I sold five copies at the bike event. There was a clown on stilts who affected a French accent. When he wasn't clowning he came over to me, rested his elbow on the van roof and chatted to me in a Geordie accent about his own camper van days.

By 8.00 on the Monday morning we had a full tank and were motoring up the M6 with the wind howling through the bars of the roof rack. Fourth gear is way over to the right and forward, pull back for fifth. On the motorway you can stay in fifth and forget about gear changing for a while. Gordon and Sandy the dog were stretched out in the back, Ringo riding shotgun in the front. He'd just got back from his Egyptian trip and was feeling the cold, ill-equipped as usual, with no warm clothes, nor waterproofs.

The weather was good to begin with. When we stopped at the Tebay services it felt balmy. It was quiet on the car-park and I felt relaxed. It didn't start raining until we got to Dumfries. The A75 takes you round the north of the city via a series of roundabouts - lots of gear changing, then it's a straight run by coast and ruined castles until you turn off on the A714 for Wigtown - Booktown, with its dozen or more bookshops.

I'd done some research into caravan sites and knew there were those who didn't accept commercial vehicles, nor single sex groups. My Transporter was a fairly low key conversion, and we were a single sex group, albeit a fairly ancient one. Would there be a problem at the campsite reception?

By the time we got to Port William the rain was lashing down, driven by a strong wind off the sea. The caravan site was right on the front, only yards from the beach. There was a caravan at one end and as far away as possible from it, a caravan at the other. There was a toilet and shower block - no office, no need to worry about a cool reception, there was no reception at all.

There was no shelter either. I parked with the back to the sea and switched off the engine. The wind rocked the van and the rain hammered on the panels. We looked at one another. Were we mad? Is this what camper-vanning's like? Ringo got his mobile out.

"I'll ring Liz."

No signal.

"Well you've got her address," I said.

He shook his head sadly and shivered.

There wasn't really room for three to sleep in the van in comfort, so we'd brought a little tent. Gordon and I donned waterproofs and faced the storm to put it up. Ringo and Sandy watched with wan interest from within.

We had a struggle with it. I hadn't put it up for years. The ground was like concrete, was concrete in fact, and the wind wanted the tent as a kite. We managed, but it didn't look right, was too squat, like an igloo in a heat-wave. It would have to do. We got back in the van and got the stove going.

It was a good cup of tea. Things slowly improved after that. Gordon did some investigating and found a notice saying someone would visit the site at four to collect payment. I tried my ancient mobile and got a signal. Ringo rang Liz and got her address. She invited us round. I lent Ringo a pullover and Gordon lent him a waterproof, and we set off. The rain was still being driven by a boisterous wind.

Liz lived on the main street. Her smart, new wood-burning stove was on the go. It was a welcome sight.

Later things improved even more. The rain stopped; the wind dropped. We readjusted the tent and made it look a bit more convincing. Ringo produced a bottle of vodka. We walked on the beach. The sea unfurled in tranquillity. Sunset effects were sketched across the western sky. At the tip of Galloway the lighthouse winked. We had dinner booked at the Clansman in Port William, which came highly recommended by Liz. The next day we planned to set off for Ayr to visit Burns' Cottage. This camper-vanning wasn't such a bad lark after all.

Closing The Book

Back in my college days there'd been much ado about local government reorganisation. The lecturers had bussed us out to meetings and conferences to carry resolutions. I hadn't understood, hadn't tried to. There were those who said libraries should be part of the education department, otherwise it would lose status, but there were those who said it would be swamped by education and would thrive better as part of leisure services.

The comings and goings of local government paralysed libraries. The engine room fell silent and the craft moved only with the tide and the wind. In 1974 Blackburn lost control of libraries to Lancashire County. Twenty years later the chance to become a unitary authority and regain them arose. Blackburn went for it.

It was 35 miles from Darwen to Lancaster before they extended the M65, a good hour each way, a couple of gallons of petrol a day. We tried to move, saw a big, pre-war semi in Heysham that we liked, but couldn't sell our house in Darwen. Parking in Lancaster was a problem too, until I got a pass for the multi-story.

One winter afternoon it started snowing there at two. The forecast was bad, so I was allowed to leave early. Unusually the snow was coming from the west. The wind that usually powered the rain, now piled in the snow, drove it in, overwhelming the vulnerable lowlands of the Lancashire plain and storming Beacon Fell. The M6 glistened blackly at first, then became furrowed with brown sludge, then became white. The traffic stopped. For two hours nothing moved on the M6. For two hours I sat in the dim snow-light, at the mercy of the blizzard. For two hours even the juggernauts marooned in the next lane could scarcely be seen for the driving snow.

When darkness fell I was still on the motorway. It was eight o clock before I crept off it and joined the crawl along the A59 to Samlesbury. It was nine before I got to Blackburn. I left the car at Ewood and walked the last few miles to Darwen past queues of standing traffic. It was ten before I got home eight hours to travel 35 miles.

In 1995 Fiona and I went our separate ways. Shortly afterwards Blackburn advertised the post of Local Studies Librarian at Darwen. Blackburn were leaving the County. Future jobs might never get advertised. It might be my last chance. I decided to go for it.

What a change to be able to walk to work. What a change to be able to get up at half past eight and still be at work on time. What a change to be home by five fifteen. Darwen Library had changed too.

In the twelve years since I'd left Blackburn had consolidated its hold. It wasn't true, as some said, that you had to ring Blackburn to get permission to go to the toilet, but Darwen's autonomy had gone. Appointing staff, dealing with leave, all financial procedures, selecting stock, all these reins of power were now in Blackburn's hands.

Bigger changes still were in the air. PCs for public use had appeared. There was a charge and they were not heavily used, but there was something called the Internet. I knew little about it and thought it was no more relevant to me than the shooting of an obscure Archduke had been to ordinary English folk 80 years earlier.

It wasn't that I was insensible to the advantages of technology. Although I'd persisted with a typewriter for a long time, I did at last buy an Amstrad word processor. It was the one Debbie in the office at Lancaster Library had used. They got rid of it, when they upgraded. I did a lot of writing on that machine. It's true the machine gun roar of the printer obliged you to leave the room when it was in full spate, and the daisy wheel stumbled over the letter 'p' and wouldn't print it, otherwise it was fine.

Great changes at Blackburn - the game was afoot. They were gearing up to join the technological revolution, to lead the technological revolution. Senior staff were being redeployed. Even I got caught up in it, being seconded to Blackburn Reference Library for the duration. After 25 years I was back where I'd started.

A major refurbishment took place. The former newspaper reading area became a 'learning zone,' a suite of PCs were installed. It was free to use them and the demand was overwhelming. There were queues all day. On the back of this success, and with money supplied by central government, a few years later, a further refurbishment convulsed the whole building. The reference library disappeared altogether, being merged with the lending library. Old ways of arranging books were abandoned, instead there were zones and themes, echoing the arrangements used in major book shops. There were self-issue stations, eye-catching displays, and dump bins.

The library was closed for several weeks while all this was done. Electricians and joiners were everywhere, and when they went at five, I appeared with a bag to collect scrap wood for the fire. There was a grand opening evening. When the old library in Library Street had opened in 1874 Gladstone had been in attendance. When it had a major refurbishment in the 1950s, Earl Attlee had officiated at the relaunch. When the new library opened in 1975 Harold Wilson did the honours. This time it was a Queen Elizabeth look-alike.

Libraries had had to do something. They'd had to reinvent themselves to survive. There were two challenges: the decline in reading and the spread of the Internet. Old people still read, but younger people did not, or if they did, got their books elsewhere. Books were relatively cheap, supermarket paperbacks anyway. The sense of community was going. People wanted new books, their own books, not ones that had been used by others, not library books. Few would clasp a grubby, dog-eared Billy Bunter book to their bosom, as I had done once. And since the arrival of the Internet, reference library use had fallen. You could find out anything you wanted to know now at the click of a mouse.

This had been brought home to me once when I was on duty with Ros, the new Reference Librarian at Blackburn. We got a request from the Children's Library for a list of kings and queens of England. I got up, intending to look in the encyclopedia and do some photocopying. Ros stayed me. She went on-line, copied a list from a reputable website and emailed it. It took her a couple of minutes. I realised then that everything had changed. I realised then that all my hard-won reference experience was no longer needed. At a time of life when I should have been at my peak, a fount of knowledge to the young and inexperienced, I was having to learn new ways. It was the young staff, whippersnappers with a couple of months' experience, who were teaching me.

Local and family history still had a role to play in this 'brave, new world.' Family history especially had become a major pursuit. Once you only did it if you had noble, or distinguished ancestors. The greater awareness of the past, fostered by TV as much as anything, the democratisation of history, meant that people realised that one person's origins were as important as anybody else's. Census and civil registration records had become more easily available. When they were only available on microfilm and microfiche, the library fairly buzzed, film and fiche readers were constantly overbooked. Later, when these resources appeared on-line, library use declined.

In 2002 a library website was launched - CottonTown. Lottery funded, it was powered along by the enthusiastic Andy Kirman and his assistant Rachel Spencer. Like Dr Who and a companion, they piloted the project back through decades and centuries of Blackburn's history, and opened up a whole new future full of possibilities for libraries. At the same time of course they were putting resources on-line, so people didn't have to visit the library to use them, a further decline in usage figures.

And so I was ending where I began - a certain symmetry in that. The library was a very different place though. The Reference Library had gone. Reference libraries all over the country were going. Now we had PCs, plasma screens, and play-stations to bring in young people. Libraries were evolving. What they were to become was impossible to say.

Yes the Reference Library had gone. It didn't matter in the end that there'd been no room for expansion when we moved from the old library. The stacks, once dense with volumes of accumulated wisdom were empty, where once thousands of voices had argued, reminisced, reasoned, rhymed, mused, prayed, and thundered were now silent, and only the faintest whispers remained.

Hair

In the bitterest weather you see them - the girls in their flimsy tops, with bare midriffs, bare shoulders and bare legs, the lads in sleeveless designer T shirts. They pay no heed to the weather. The icy blast can be barbed with snow, but they'll turn out in outfits more suited to hot summer nights.

How different it was years ago. Then, if it was chilly, your Mum wouldn't let you leave the house without your gaberdine raincoat, balaclava and gloves, with the ends of your scarf spread solicitously across your chest. 'Wrap up.' 'Keep your back warm.' 'Put something on your head.' These were the exhortations from a generation who remembered the days before antibiotics, when contempt for the weather could lead to a chill and death. Victorian novels abound with examples of tragedy brought about by being caught unprepared in a downpour. Lingering too long at the graveside of a relative in inclement weather could mean it would soon be opened up again - for you.

Try suggesting to your kids today, when they're getting ready to go out, that they should wear a jumper, or take a scarf, or put gloves on. They'll look at you as though you're quite mad. They want to look right, look good, look like their mates. They want to look cool, even if that means being cold. When did it start this obsession with image?

The first clothes I remember were short pants made out of green corduroy. We had an endless supply of green corduroy, which Dad brought home from the mill and Mum made into pants. All boys wore short pants and had the scarred and grimy knees to prove it. I was the last in my class to go into long trousers, when I was thirteen.

My problem with clothes was that they were uncomfortable rather than unfashionable. When I was seven I had a leather, or leatherette, helmet that buckled under the chin and chafed cruelly. Shoes always pinched, especially with Mum's knitted socks on. Mum was a formidable knitter: socks, gloves, scarves, cardigans, jumpers. After every wash the sleeves would get longer and longer. They had to be rolled up so that my stick-thin wrists could emerge. Dad had no sympathy for complaints about shoes hurting. 'They'll soon shape to fit your feet, when I was a lad we had clogs, and your feet had to shape to fit your clogs.' I couldn't tie shoelaces, so on days when we did PT, I went to school in my pumps, so I didn't have to change.

At Grange Grammar School we had uniforms: navy blue blazers, caps, white shirts and ties and navy blue gaberdines. Wearing it and seeing it hung up in your bedroom made school seem all pervasive, made it seem to dominate your life. For the first time I was wearing clothes that represented something, rather than just being functional. Of course my clothes had always said a lot about me, about my class, about my parents income, about the age I lived in, but I didn't know that. Everybody I knew wore the same kind of clothes.

Until quite recently clothes had been a give away about origin and status. In Edwardian times the destitute wore rags; the workers wore clogs, shawls and mufflers; the middle classes sported bowlers; the toffs wore toppers and flourished silver-topped canes. Well-to-do women sailed along in silks and satins, with elaborate bonnets and veils. A glance would tell you where someone belonged. And then came two wars and universal conscription.

In the army you were clean-shaven, with your hair cut short at the back and sides, and you wore a uniform. This carried over into civilian life; a sober suit and shirt and tie became the universal uniform, and everybody had short hair. Only the cut and quality of your suit betrayed your class. For women there was less uniformity. The upper classes were still butterflies compared to the dowdy moths of the lower orders.

The Teddy Boys of the 1950s rebelled flamboyantly against uniformity, wearing bright colours, sculpting their hair and growing sideburns, but it was in the 1960s that the revolution against suits and short back and sides really began, when, all over the land, fathers were suddenly aghast at what their sons had become. Every time I appeared I wiped the smile off my Dad's face.

I have to say though the first man I ever saw with a beard and shoulder-length hair was my Uncle Peter, Mum's brother, and that was back in the 1950s. Peter lived with my Granddad Lorenzo. My Grandma Alice had been dead many years. I never knew her. The two of them lived in spectacular squalor off Manningham Lane, near the old Bradford City football ground. The dust lay so thick on the floor, you left footprints in it. Newspaper at the windows served as a curtain. Newspaper on the table served as a cloth. Dad would never go there, and when me and Mum did, Peter, who spent his days reading paperbacks, would go upstairs until we'd gone. When Lorenzo died, Peter abandoned his home and started sleeping rough. He was found dead in a derelict house a few years later.

The 1960s were well under way, and I was still in my school

uniform. It was showing signs of wear and tear. My raincoat was beltless and seldom buttoned up. My tie was askew. I'd lost my cap. My shoes were scuffed and unpolished. My hair rarely saw the attention of a brush. I could have made a passable William Brown. There were scores like me at school, but increasingly there were boys who were changing. They wore long pants, and not flapping flannels either, but tailored ones, made narrower by obliging Mums. They'd swapped their gaberdines for stylish, short, white macs. Instead of sensible shoes, they wore pointed ones - winklepickers. They spent time cultivating their quiffs. I didn't understand. I scorned them, but as the months went by, there were more like them and fewer like me.

The 1960s revolution was heralded by a joyous, jangling chord that roared out from the mouth of the Cavern Club in Liverpool. The Beatles were here and popular music, fashion, teenage life were never going to be the same again. Kids were wearing Beatle jackets, tight jeans, Chelsea boots and letting their hair grow. The Rolling Stones appeared with hair almost down to the collar, and caused apoplexy in the older generations. It was a time for experiment and individuality. Industry and advertising had not yet imposed the uniformity that was to come later.

At school signs of the revolution were fairly muted, but there were rebels. Eddie Grice, a formidable, bare-foot cross-country runner let his long, black locks flow in his slipstream. Headmaster Tebbitt tried to shame him by pinning up photos with facetious captions about him looking like a girl. Nobody, but nobody could mistake Eddie Grice for a girl. Music teacher Mr Rhodes made a similar Canute-like stance, sending letters to parents asking them to stop their children listening to popular music.

I wanted to be part of it all. I wasn't sure about Beatle jackets and Cuban-heeled boots, even then I could see that that was swapping one uniform for another, but I wanted to emerge from my chrysalis, spread my wings. Not much I could do with the 62p I got for my paper round every week, and Dad certainly wasn't going to fork out for anything that wasn't sombre, sensible and conventional. All I could do was grow my hair.

I'd never liked going to the barber's, not even to Reggie Holland's in Chapel Street in Queensbury when I was four - and he gave you a balloon, if you were brave. Back in the 1950s barbers were always full. You always had to queue, and there was always the danger that a little boy's place in the queue might not be acknowledged. And then there was the haircutting itself - the razor going up the back of your head, the unwanted intimacy with the barber, the pummelling of your head with Brylcreem, the performance at the end with the mirrors, when you were supposed to express your satisfaction. I always escaped into the cold like a sheep fleeing naked from the shearer. But it wasn't that. I wanted to grow my hair to be me.

It's easy to say that it was the hair that caused all the rows between me and Dad; there were many other things. We saw the world in different ways. Hair was the big issue of the day though. Keith, a friend of mine from York, turned up at his digs in Leeds, and the landlady wouldn't let him in the house because he had long hair. Another friend, Tony, was walking down the street when an old guy started belabouring him with his walking stick because he had long hair. Not being served in pubs and cafes was routine. We were dangerous. We were shunned. We lived on the edge. It gave us an inkling of what it was like to be black, and you couldn't get much cooler than that back in the late 1960s.

At college you could wear what you wanted, and in the common room you could see full-blooded hippies, with beads, dyed grandad vests, loon pants and sandals; long-haired types in Army great-coats and pumps; and chaps in suits and ties. All kinds of compromises were represented too. My flat-mate Richard had started college in sports jacket and cravat. He grew his hair long and bought an Afghan jacket, but he kept the cravat and his Hush Puppies.

Having long hair and a beard was enough for me. I'd neither the cash, nor the confidence to follow fashion. I favoured the functional - more Famous Army Stores and Millets, than Carnaby

Street and the Portobello Road. Waiting for the bus one night, I was surrounded by a gang of skinheads, who wanted confirmation that I was a hippie before they beat me up. I refused to be categorised, and before they could resolve the dilemma, the bus came and I made my escape.

My appearance changed when I met Penny. Old fashioned underpants and string vests were out. Out too went old jumpers and combat boots. In were slim-fitting shirts and flares, and casual, corduroy jackets. By the time I started work, employers had become fairly relaxed about dress - jumpers and jeans were just about OK, but the ambitious still wore suits and ties.

By the time my own children, William and Emily, were growing up, teenage clothes were big business. It was very important to be wearing the right brand names. You wasted your breath trying to persuade them to accept cheaper alternatives. In vain did you point out to them that they were being manipulated, duped by global corporations. No, they had to be wearing Nike, or Adidas, or Kappa, or they'd be pariahs, shunned by their fellows.

The young apart, anything goes now. Although the suit and tie is still the favoured uniform of people in power all over the world, you can see millionaire-entrepreneurs in jumpers and jeans. Anything goes. You can see old men and young men in trainers and track suits, the baseball cap has become the headgear of choice for the simple minded of all ages, and tattoos and piercings are commonplace.

Today kids can dye their hair any colour they want, have it all sorts of different colours, make it spiky, have it down to their waists, shave it off - and nobody notices. It must be so frustrating. As for me, well there's a definite drift back to the William Brown look. I have to guard against the wishful thinking, common to many aging men who live alone, that the grimy collar, frayed cuffs, and odd soup stain won't be noticed, or, what's even worse, that it doesn't matter, that people will think your mind must be on loftier matters. I have to force myself to shave, wash, and remember to polish my shoes, and as for my hair, well now it's like the

December twilight - grey, lifeless and very short.

Snowing like Billy-Ho

I've heard Dad talk about the great winter of '47 so much that I've come to think I remember it myself.

It snowed for three days and three nights without stopping. When you opened your front door, you had to cut steps in the snow to get to the top of the drift, and when you walked along it, you could bend down and touch the tops of the lamp posts. There was a tram stuck at Littlemoor on the border between Bradford and Queensbury, and folk went in at one end and out the other to get through the drift.

An inch or two of snow today causes no end of problems - traffic is grid-locked, trains can't operate, schools close. Fifty years ago a couple of feet of snow didn't cause any problems. Kids walked to school anyway. Folk walked to work. The shop was on the corner. Everybody you wanted to visit was within walking distance. There were plenty of ashes from the fire to throw on the ice, and everybody cleared the snow away from their own front door.

When local government reorganisation tampered with the Yorkshire/Lancashire boundaries, an old Todmordener was asked what she thought of coming under the 'White Rose.' "I'm not keen - they have terrible winters in Yorkshire," she said.

It's true there seemed to be more snow growing up in Yorkshire than I've experienced since living in Lancashire. More snow, but never enough, never ever enough.

Eskimos are said to have many different words for snow. Living in Lancashire, you might think we'd have lots of words for rain, but we don't, nor do we have words to differentiate the different types of snow. The big, fluffy, picture-book stuff, with flakes the size of a cat's paw looks so good descending, but doesn't last. It soon turns to rain. Better when the rain itself turns to snow, when the driving, grey rain suddenly has tracers of snow in it. When its straight, slanting lines suddenly stray, falter, begin to swoop and flock. Best of all though is the fine, hard snow that sweeps along like blown sand, and finds gaps in windows and skylights, and accumulates relentlessly, sculpting elegant drifts that overtop walls and fences and span lanes, roads and motorways.

How the world changes when it's white over and the air is full of white descending. The human mind loves this transformation. The canine mind too - dogs plough the snow up with their snouts, roll in it, and leap to snatch at snowballs. Maybe not the feline mind - cats step disdainfully, picking their way with twitching tails, and certainly not the avian mind - birds huddle, fluffed up, on telegraph wires, viewing with dismay their diminishing food prospects.

How magical the snow-filled night is, how silent, how numinous. Your breath haunts the air. Each step crumps crisply. Behind, your track curves into the past. Ahead, unblemished, the white field merges into the dark blue cloisters of the snow-bound forest. Frost crystals spark randomly, mirroring the stars. Anything can happen. Every moment is full of magic.

It's a magic that seldom survives the dawn though. Melting snow drips from the eaves, and what remains on the ground is shrunken and disfigured by a thousand footprints. But not always...

One day maybe I'll talk about the winter of 1962/63 in the same way Dad talked about '47. The snow started on Christmas Day in Scotland, giving Glasgow its first white Christmas since 1938, but didn't reach us until Boxing Day. Mum, Dad and Linda went off to the Sutcliffes. I didn't go. I had two school friends coming round, Andy Jowett and Ian Booth, and Andy had promised to bring some rum. I'd become something of a connoisseur of rum. Captain Morgan was best, though Lambs was OK. I didn't like Lemon Heart. Yates Wine Lodge did a 100 proof rum, though it was to be a couple of years later, when I was working before I sampled that. Spirits were expensive then; £20 a bottle at today's prices.

Andy kept his promise, and brought some beer as well. The rum was Dark Fire, a local brewery brand. I remember being out in the snow, skylarking and being silly, but I was too drunk to appreciate the magic of it. Later I had the novel experience of being sick at the same time as I was falling down the stairs. Andy and Ian helped to make me presentable, but I was a poor creature cowering by the hearth when Mum and Dad returned. 'Upset stomach,' I whimpered. Dad wasn't convinced, but the snow covered my tracks. They were full of their perilous bus journey down from Queensbury. I crept to the window and looked out at the blizzard, a white maelstrom that should have roared in its ferocity but was silent. Pale as the landscape was, I was paler.

It snowed all night and the morning brought no thaw, but more snow. England was white from north to south, even the Channel Isles were blanketed. In the south-west drifts approaching twenty feet left villages cut off, disrupted road and rail travel and prevented farmers reaching livestock. It was the start of the coldest winter since 1740, with temperatures five degrees below average all through January. After the initial shock people got on with it. I walked to school. Dad walked to work. Mum walked to the shops. Everybody just got on with it.

On a bitter Friday night at the end of January a Liverpool band loaded their instruments into the van and braved the icy roads of Lancashire. They were on their way to Darwen to play at a Scout dance at the Co-operative Hall. There must have been one or two comments about the disagreeableness of it all and the temptation to just not turn up must have been great. After all their single 'Love me Do' had just reached number seventeen in the charts.

The snow persisted - day after day, week after week, month after month it persisted. My sister Linda threw some money into the snow from her bedroom window at the beginning of January, and it was to be a long time before she saw it again. The eye became used to the whiteness, and when in March the thaw began, it was a shock to see green again, even the anaemic yellow-green of grass that had lain under ice and snow for months.

There's been nothing like it since. Many's the time I've scanned the winter skies, looking for that slate-grey cloud that smothers the sun and presages snow. Winters have come and gone without a flurry. There have been white interludes, mornings when the bedroom has been lit in that particular way snow brings; crawlings home from work when tea-time snow has disrupted traffic; episodes of gently falling snow, which have tantalised and then faded, haunting refrains that have never quite developed.

Not as much chance of snow in Lancashire, but if there is any it's as likely to fall in Darwen as anywhere else; the Circus is 600 feet above sea-level. There can be snow lying in Darwen, when there's none at all in Blackburn, though Billinge Hill and distant Pendle sometimes has a white winter coat. In recent years having to drive back to Yorkshire every week to see Mum and Dad, who are back in Queensbury, has given me an equivocal attitude - not much fun braving the Pennines in a blizzard when you know anxious parents are peering with dismay at worsening road conditions.

But if you don't need to stir, if the fire's burning brightly, and your vodka's chilling in the fridge, there's nothing better than to look out at a white world, and see the snow coming down like

Billy-ho.

It Doesn't Feel Like Christmas...

Christmas has been hijacked at least twice. The first time by the Christians who gave it its present name, and the second time by commercial concerns. The Christians grafted their celebration on to an already long established sacred time. As the developed world grew prosperous, commercial interests seized on Christmas as an opportunity to sell more goods and services.

On June 21st in my first year at Hollands Cottage, I chiselled an arrow on the perimeter wall of the outbuildings, aimed at the point where the sun disappeared over the horizon at dusk. Six months later on the 21st of December I made a similar mark. I was surprised at the angle between the two - 90 degrees, one quarter of the horizon. Early Earth dwellers, who had time and good reason to observe natural phenomena must have grown alarmed as the Sun dwindled and the powers of darkness grew.

Even today when we can banish darkness at the flick of a switch, when homes are centrally heated, when brightly lit screens animate our living spaces and provide entertainment, even today the days of December bring darkness and despair.

As I write I feel all is ebbing, an upset stomach and a cold provide a backdrop of low key misery. We've had some hard frosts, and the car won't start when the temperature gets below freezing. It's a diesel, a Renault Clio. Diesels take some starting, and batteries lose 50% of their power when the ice takes a grip. The central heating has packed in and the severe frost has caused taps in the bathroom to spring leaks. The shower isn't working. The fluorescent light is on the blink, literally. Fumes and smoke from the living room fire are escaping into my bedroom. It seems that whichever way I turn things are falling apart. Entropy reigns.

How much bleaker for early men and women! When the sun set, sixteen hours of darkness lay before them, sixteen hours in a cave, or primitive shelter; sixteen hours with little or no fire: finding fuel to sustain a fire night after night would have been a hard task; sixteen hours with little or nothing to eat: hunting would have been difficult with small mammals hibernating, and wolves and bear and big cats competing for larger game. Indeed the ferocity of these predators would have been be sharpened by the harsh conditions and humans would have become a more attractive food source. There may well have been too a racial memory of the last Ice Age, when summer never came back and many perished in the terrible beauty of eternal winter

Little wonder then that means were devised to observe the position of the sun, that standing stones were erected and carefully positioned. And when the elders, those early astronomers, verified that the Sun's decline was arrested, that it was about to return, little wonder that the news was seized upon with great joy and a season of feasting and celebration followed. Unlike now when a mere day is allocated, the old Yule saw more than a month of great fires and feasting, so that when it was all over at last, when the celebrants emerged groggily from their hangovers, the days were longer, the sun was stronger and the green shoots of new growth were showing. Even in the Christian era Christmas lasted longer, ending on Candlemas, the 2nd of February. When agriculture became more organised, this was cut back, and Christmas ended on January 6th, Epiphany. The first Monday after Epiphany was known as Plough Monday.

There wasn't an awful lot to do in late December and January in agricultural communities, but industrialisation changed all that. Machines could not stand idle. The long winter break vanished and folk were lucky if they got Christmas Day off. These days the holiday has expanded and many people get two or three days, or even a week, but it still doesn't do justice to the season, or the effect of the cold and the dark on people who live in northern latitudes. We need a month at this time of year to sleep, to daydream, to plan feasts and recover from them. You could choose your own Christmas Day. There'd be plenty time to see everybody and have that week away in a remote cottage. But of course it can't be done now; our lives are too complex and high-tec. If your central heating boiler breaks down on the 24th of December, you don't want to be told that the heating engineer won't be back at work till Candlemas.

Extravagant expenditure at Christmas time is a recent phenomenon, although folk would do their best with meagre means. There wasn't much point in advertisers targeting ordinary people, they'd nothing to spend. The only credit available was the slate at the corner shop - two ounce of beef dripping till pay day. Now with people owing thousands to the student loan company, tens of thousands to credit card companies and hundreds of thousands to building societies and banks, a few extra hundred spent at Christmas time is neither here nor there. Thus the advertising onslaught starts in late summer and builds to a frenzy of shopping in the week before Christmas - chaos on the supermarket car-parks and fisticuffs over the smoked salmon in Marks and Spencers. It's as though months of bleak weather and famine threatened, whereas the shops are open again on Boxing Day.

I stand back, stand aloof from the melee. I have to shop, but do it by stealth, buying a few items now and again, or going late, or early when it's quieter. You can go as early as you like on Christmas Eve though and the car-park will be full. The point of Christmas seems to get lost in all this activity. You glimpse it sometimes, driving on country lanes on still December days, when the hedgerows have that purple cast and the black fields are frozen. Often you don't notice it at all until afterwards when you look back, and that night you drove out to friends to exchange gifts a few days before Christmas suddenly seems full of the Christmas spirit, and it fills you with poignant nostalgia and regret that you didn't realise it at the time. Or it can be something more mundane like going to the garage on the morning of Christmas Eve to have a puncture repaired, hearing carols on the mechanics' radio and listening to their banter and Christmas plans. Christmas rushes relentlessly towards you. It comes and goes before you can grasp it.

This year I put out a selection of literature: my treasured copy of 'A Christmas Carol,' illustrated by Ronald Searle, 'Pickwick Papers,' with a book mark in the Christmas at Dingley Dell chapter, Agatha Christie's 'Adventures of a Christmas Pudding,' 'Billy Bunter's Christmas' etc., thinking that in leisure moments people would select a volume and have a quiet read, but there are no such leisure moments. Everything's so frantic: shopping, more shopping, shopping again for last minute things; cooking, endless cooking, washing-up, endless washing-up; driving here, driving there; trying to visit everybody, to deliver all the presents; looking after whoever's ill - there's always somebody ill at Christmas.

What I had in mind was how it was for the leisured wealthy once, and maybe still is, when there were servants to do the work and all the guests had to do was stroll around the grounds working up an appetite for the next meal, or, if the weather turned bitter and snow threatened, spend an hour or so by the library fire with a seasonal volume, lifting their gaze now and then to the french windows and the deer park beyond where the first flakes of snow were flying on the wind.

If the snow continued, if it settled and became deep enough. If it came down handsomely and a freeze set in, then there'd be skating parties on the lake, snowballing, sledging and the sculpting of snowmen. Then in the December darkness they'd return to the country house whose windows would be all aglow, to hand their sodden, snow-mantled garments to indulgent servants before gathering by the blazing yule log fire in the great hall to drink mulled wine, or hot pineapple-rum.

Our modern, reduced Christmas leaves no time for such frivolity, let alone time for reverie and contemplation. No wonder, after the Christmas dinner is over, the dish washer full and set about its business, no wonder, as you slump supine and stuffed in front of the TV, overcome with lassitude, no wonder, as you look out at the muggy, grey weather and wonder when you should start tea, no wonder you say to yourself - 'it doesn't feel like Christmas.'

Endings and Beginnings

Five o clock on a bitter, late November morning, but the petrol station forecourt was brightly lit and surprisingly busy, with burly workmen in fluorescent jackets picking up chocolate bars and their copies of the Sun.

I filled the van up to the brim - £57 worth. You couldn't have squeezed in another drop, not enough to get a flame out of a cigarette lighter. Ringo had his Guardian for the crossword. Gordon had a bottle of milk for our brews later in the day. We all piled aboard. Sandy reluctantly conceding the seat to Gordon and then scrabbling back on to his knee. I started her up, switched on the headlights, and the engine died. I tried to fire her up again - nothing, just a click. I exchanged glances with Gordon. I tried again - nothing, just a click. It was the click of a switch in a dark room, with no bulb in the socket.

Our second van trip - the Yorkshire coast, Withernsea first, and then northward to Whitby. The original plan had been to set off the night before at 8.00 when I got home from work, but Ringo had vetoed this on the grounds that we'd be trawling around all night, looking for somewhere to stop. He didn't think much of my suggestion that we stay on the car-park of Hull's 24 hour Tesco on Beverley Road.

"You won't be able to have a drink," he warned. "The police'll move us on."

It was a clinching argument. I insisted on an early start though, so we set our alarms for 4.30. We were awoken well before by other alarms, by an eldritch screech which pierced the dark. We'd remained in the dark for some more moments, until it emerged that Gordon had been stung on the neck by a wasp - an unusual occurrence at 3.00 in the morning near the end of November, but then the autumn had been warm and insects had persisted, as had the leaves on the trees.

I'm not at my sharpest at 5.00 in the morning and I had a bit of a hangover. I stared at the ignition, wondering what to do. I switched off the lights and tried again. It fired up.

"Don't put the lights on. Let it run," Ringo warned.

"I'll just get away from the pumps," I said, and rolled round the side of the garage. We were only a couple of hundred yards away from home, on a brightly-lit main road. I decided to risk driving back and was just about to do so, when a police car came on to the forecourt. The officer got out and went inside. I couldn't risk it now, not with goodness knows how much alcohol still sloshing around my blood stream from the night before. I thought, 'He'll not be long, just calling for a chocolate bar and a Coke.'

Fifteen minutes later, he was still inside. This wasn't how it was supposed to be. We should have been well on our way along the M62 by now. I was just on the point of risking it anyway, when he came out and drove away. As soon as he was out of sight, I drove out of the garage. Cars coming the other way flashed at us, but we gained the safety of Hollands Cottage.

The engine had been running all this time. I tried the lights again. They came on. The engine was still running.

"What do we do?" I asked.

"It'll be your battery," Ringo said. "You've not been using it recently."

"Supposing it's something else," I said, not fancying getting stranded on the M62 in the morning rush hour.

"Let's go. We're in the RAC," he said.

I looked at Gordon, who reserved his judgement. Sandy looked eager, ready to be off.

"OK, let's go," I said and we rolled back out on to the main road.

I'd made a few changes to the van since the Scottish trip; bought a leisure battery and a portable TV; bought a paraffin heater - a monster that filled the van with soporific heat; bought an electric lamp at great expense that was supposed to floodlight the whole van, but which just produced a not too helpful, blue glow. The van had become a preoccupation. I spent a lot of time planning improvements, planning trips.

In the darkness before dawn it was busy on the M62. When Bradford and Leeds loomed the red lights ahead bunched up and we crawled, and then stopped, and then crawled, and stopped again. And so it was, until we got past the exit for the M1 and the red lights spread out a bit.

We were driving east, and there were pale fissures in the blackness up ahead, but it wasn't until we were on the A63 approaching Hull, that another day had unequivocally dawned. We had a toilet break at the Little Chef and then joined the morning rush-hour. We passed the Humber Bridge and the docks, and then got on the A1033. A large van loomed up behind and stuck with us all the way to Withernsea.

I was last here in 1971 after marrying Penny. Her Dad had a workmate who had a caravan here. I remember the evenings - pints of Guinness and walks back to the caravan along the front, with the fringe of foam, slightly luminous in the darkness, and the sound of its dying sigh. I'd been here before with Mum, Dad and

Linda, in the days when there were trains from Hull. We'd walked round and round the few shops, until we knew every item on display.

More shops now and a bit of a pre-Christmas bustle. We parked on the front and walked through the castellated gateway down on to the sands. One or two were exercising their dogs. It was bright, and a big, bold wind had the sea roaring in. Out there, a mile out there, were the drowned ruins of a church. The sea continually erodes this coast and seemed to have an appetite today for another chunk. We had an appetite for breakfast.

Just as the shoreline becomes littered with flotsam and jetsam, the rubbish of holiday-makers and passing shipping, so seaside towns attract emporia selling cheap trash: everything from brands of soap powder that nobody's ever heard of, to 100 piece socket sets for 99p, the kind of shops where, if you'd saved the owner's life and he said you could help yourself, you'd come out empty-handed. Withernsea has lots of these establishments, well patronised by pale, fat people.

We made our way up the coast on roads that bent, seemingly needlessly, back and forth; there were no hills to avoid. We followed up all the camping site signs, but they were all closed. We reached Filey. It was busy and hard to park. Once November Filey would have been deserted but for seagulls, and lone shoppers scurrying before the wind, now affluent pensioners keep the tourist industry going all year round. The Tourist Information Office wasn't open though, so no opportunity to enquire about camping sites.

I came to Filey in 1977 with Tony and Linda and their son John. We had a caravan at Primrose Valley. I'd been at school with Tony, though he was a year older, so we didn't get to know each other till we'd both left. I met Linda at the party where she and Tony met. You'd not find a friendlier person than Linda, but if she feels she's not getting her dues, then you'll not meet anyone more formidable.

We arrived in Tony's Mini. There was a long wait for keys.

When we got our caravan at last, Linda was not happy. It certainly was a bit grubby, but me and Tony would have put up with it.

"Tony, it's disgusting! They've not cleaned. We're not staying here." Linda declared.

She marched back to reception and shortly afterwards we were allocated a caravan that had never been used, a brand new one.

Years later Fiona and I stayed at a bungalow at Filey. Oddly enough that was none too clean either, and, odder still, the landlady complained at the end of the week that we'd not kept it tidy. Maybe it was a defence strategy.

The caravan park at North Cliff County Park above Filey was closed and the Caravan Club one on the A1039 out of town couldn't accommodate us. I don't think they liked the look of us - an old van with its home-made top box, three desperados and a tinker's cur are not what most site owners want to see turning in at their gate.

It was after three, and we wanted to be parked up somewhere before it got dark at about 4.30. There was a campsite at Cayton and one or two on the A170 Pickering road. If those failed us, I thought we could drive up into Dalby Forest and find a quiet spot. I warned the others that there'd be no facilities though, no pubs, no shops, nowhere to get food. They looked alarmed and began to take a more serious interest in the map.

Cayton campsite was closed. We weren't very far from Cayton Bay, where we'd had the caravan holiday with Sutcliffe, not far in miles, but a million light years away from who I was then, and the way of life I'd led. We passed a bungalow in Cayton village where Fiona and I had stayed once. We had William, and her Mum, Marianne, had been there. William was in a travelling cot and kept climbing out and falling on the floor.

The camp at Wykeham was closed. We turned down a narrow lane at Snainton to White House Farm. There was no sign of life, so we turned back for the main road. I decided we'd try the one at Allerston, and then give it up and head for the woods. It was another narrow lane to Carr House Farm. I didn't have high hopes.

It was still daylight, but it was a faltering light, a waning light. The first breath of night would snuff it out.

When the entrance came into view, I was all ready to begin a see-sawing turn, but the gate was open. I drove through. The door at reception was open too, and there was somebody manning the counter. It was open. I think they were as pleased to see us, as we were to see them; we were the only ones on the site.

Coats, bedding, sleeping bags, newspapers and maps were all piled up in the back of the van. It was a job to get to the box where the tea-making apparatus was. I decided I'd have to arrange things better. I needed a rack for newspapers, maps and books, and a shelf for mugs and the kettle and tea and coffee, hooks for coats etc - something to think about during the long winter nights to come.

We had a brew, put the tent up, and set off for the nearest pub, a mile up the lane. It was cold, seriously cold. There was a full moon. It was an enchanted walk. We were like sprites, Jack Frosts, peering in at windows. We fortified ourselves with nips of vodka. The windows of the cottages glowed pleasantly - glimpses of bright coal fires and children just in from school, with the flickering reflection of TVs on their faces.

We had a drink in the Cayley Arms. The barman came round and made the fire blaze for us. Then we walked down the road to Ebberston, a perilous journey with no pavement, no light, and the tea-time traffic streaming past. We reached the Foxholme Hotel, just as it was opening. There were quite a few there, even so early, but it was the darts team assembling before setting off for an away match. After they'd gone it was empty. We walked back to the Cayley Arms and ordered dinner.

Afterwards we walked back to the campsite, got the paraffin stove going, put the TV on and had a pleasant hour in a soporific warmth, topping up our good spirits with bad ones - cheap vodka. At the point when Ringo became convinced that there were four of us and started showing concern for the missing one, we decided to call it a day and despatched him to his tent to face the minus three temperature

On the Wednesday morning we headed for Whitby, climbing the North York Moors, and it was a climb, down to first gear up some of the banks, in the wake of struggling coaches. Whitby was busy. The Tourist Information Office was full of elderly people. Of course we weren't much younger ourselves. We were all old fogeys together, enjoying the last of the summer wine.

Whitby's a town of many levels. There's the seaside trashy shop phenomenon, but there are more elevated establishments - classy shops selling artwork and Whitby jet and curios. There's geological Whitby with fossils and dinosaur remains. There's historic Whitby with Captain Cook associations. There's literary Whitby, gothic Whitby with Dracula and the ruined abbey. There's quayside Whitby with its cafes and souvenir shops, and there's cliff-top Whitby, with cottages braving the North Sea wind.

After breakfast we climbed up to the interesting shops, and descended the other side to the harbour and beach, where the sea roared in, stoked up by the wind.

And that's where I'll leave us. This is where the book ends - this ragbag of reminiscence and reconstruction. I'll end it here at the point where we were looking out at the great white rollers being combed out of the turbulent grey sea.

It's tempting to speculate, to extrapolate, to talk of the future, to look forward to new horizons, new adventures, but that would be tempting to fate too. Who knows what will happen? All there really is is now. We all wish our lives away. We all want this minute to pass, thinking a better one is coming. So often people sacrifice the now for a future when they'll have what they've always dreamed of, always worked towards - the villa in Crete, the apartment in Spain, the country cottage in Scotland, then they'll be happy. It's human nature to plan and strive and look to the future. It's an evolutionary thing, a technique for survival, but evolution doesn't care if the villa in Crete turns out not to be paradise, or if life in a Scottish cottage turns out to be much like life has always been, except lonelier.

No, when we get to the end of the road at last, when the illusion of time collapses, telescopes, dwindles, when we get to the very end, then we'll know that the moment is all there is, all there ever was, and all there ever will be - magic, or not.